PROPS FOR

Bryant Terry's *The Inspired Vegan*

"Bryant Terry is a culinary muse unlike any other. Of course, this book is filled with delicious, unexpected, and exciting recipes. But they're seasoned with uplifting history, powerful music, beautiful ideas, sweet memories, and deep compassion. Bryant's great gift is to reconnect us with the radical joy that food brings, making inspired vegans out of us all."

—Raj Patel, author of *The Value of Nothing* and *Stuffed and Starved*

"Bryant Terry has crafted a cuisine that is vivid, colorful, and uniquely American. He seamlessly blends the food traditions of the African diaspora with the farm-to-table freshness of Northern California. Sweet and sensuous, rich and refreshing, his mouthwatering dishes jump off the page."

—Louisa Shafia, chef and author of
Lucid Food: Cooking for an Eco-Conscious Life

"I stopped by Bryant Terry's place in Oakland when he was writing *The Inspired Vegan*. I found greens in the garden, something delicious in the kitchen, and in him, an inspiring commitment to bettering the world by bringing people together around soulful food. Reading this book is like spending the afternoon with him all over again."

—Josh Viertel, president, Slow Food USA

"In *The Inspired Vegan*, Bryant Terry's exuberant, healthful, and playful remix of African American, West African, Chinese, and other cultural cuisines is deftly matched by his bold progressive thinking and storytelling."

—Didi Emmons, chef and author of *Wild Flavors*

"*The Inspired Vegan* is like a personal journal where readers get an intimate perspective into Bryant's inspired world. He strives to build awareness, culture, and community through food, and this latest book does so in a simply delicious manner. "

—Aida Mollenkamp, Food Writer and Chef

"*The Inspired Vegan* is incredibly dope. This beautiful book not only changes the way we see and taste food, it changes the way we see and taste the world. *The Inspired Vegan*, like gumbo, is a delicious collage of ingredients: recipes, art, culture, inspiration, and social change. Enlightening, uplifting, and hungering, *The Inspired Vegan* is a must read and a must taste."

—MK Asante, author, filmmaker, professor

"*The Inspired Vegan* melts my heart. I'm in love with Terry's beautifully crafted book, and readers will enjoy healthful and tasty treats, such as Sweet Potato-Cornmeal Drop Biscuits (to the tune of "Steal Away" by Mahalia Jackson), and agave-sweetened Mexican Chocolate Pudding, inspired by Cynthia Well's *Colores de la Vida*. This book will stay on your kitchen shelves for years."

—A. Breeze Harper, The Sistah Vegan Project

the inspired vegan

Books by Bryant Terry

*Vegan Soul Kitchen: Fresh, Healthy,
and Creative African-American Cuisine*

Grub: Ideas for an Urban Organic Kitchen
(with Anna Lappé)

the inspired vegan

seasonal ingredients
creative recipes
mouthwatering menus

Bryant Terry

Da Capo
LIFE
LONG

A MEMBER OF PERSEUS BOOKS GROUP

Designed by Timm Bryson
Set in 11 point Arno Pro by the Perseus Books Group

Cataloging-in-Publication data for this book is available from the Library of Congress.
First Da Capo Press edition 2012
ISBN 978-0-7382-1375-0
ISBN 978-0-7382-1547-1 (e-book)

Published by Da Capo Press
A Member of the Perseus Books Group
www.dacapopress.com

Da Capo Press books are available at special discounts for bulk purchases in the U.S. by corporations, institutions, and other organizations. For more information, please contact the Special Markets Department at the Perseus Books Group, 2300 Chestnut Street, Suite 200, Philadelphia, PA 19103, or call (800) 810-4145, ext. 5000, or e-mail special.markets@perseusbooks.com.

10 9 8 7 6 5 4 3 2 1

For Jidan and Mila
(R.I.P. Maholi)

contents

menus 37

autumn

introduction

start

In 2007, shortly after moving to the Bay Area from Brooklyn, I lived across the street from Lake Merritt—a beautiful body of water adjacent to downtown Oakland. Every day of the week, I had easy access to a plethora of healthy food options. My apartment was just two blocks from a well-stocked, independently owned health food store that offered a variety of organic, fresh fruits and vegetables, as well as bulk grains and beans. I could also walk to the new 40,000-square-foot Whole Foods Market, which sold everything imaginable (insert side-eye). On Saturdays, I'd stroll to the Grand Lake Farmers' Market, which hosted forty-four local farmers, thirty specialty food purveyors, and a handful of local artisans.

I lived in a food paradise—which made it difficult to fathom how there could be a food desert (as it is often described) so close by. Just about a mile and a half from Whole Foods is the community of West Oakland, which in 2007 was home to fifty-three liquor stores and not one full-service supermarket. Let me repeat that: Liquor stores: 53 / Supermarkets: 0. Many of the thirty thousand residents (primarily African American) living in that neighborhood did not own cars, and it was incredibly difficult for them to travel to other parts of Oakland, or to Emeryville or Berkeley to shop for food. As a result, folks relied upon the liquor/convenience stores to meet their grocery needs. It goes without saying that those stores sold very few, if any, fresh fruits and vegetables, and what food they did offer tended to be processed.

Unfortunately, across the country, there are far too many communities like West Oakland, where people are denied the basic human right to healthful, safe, affordable, and culturally appropriate food. Not surprisingly, these communities have some of the highest rates of obesity and diet-related ill-nesses in the nation. To combat this injustice, a number of organizations, proj-ects, and individuals have been working tirelessly to create community-based solutions for producing food in an affordable, sustainable, and eco-friendly manner while teaching people how to select ingredients and prepare whole-some meals for themselves and their families. Following on my background as a grassroots activist, I see my work as a chef and author contributing to one of the most hopeful movements of the twenty-first century—food justice!

In fact, this year is special for me, as it marks my tenth anniversary working to create a healthy, just, and sustainable food system. A decade ago I started dreaming of ways to make fresh, affordable food more widely accessible, which would help eliminate health disparities between low-income and higher-income people living in cities. I enrolled in the Natural Gourmet In-stitute for Health & Culinary Arts with the express purpose of gaining the skills to start a project that would educate young people about healthy cook-ing and food politics while empowering them to become peer educators and food justice activists. Soon after graduating, I founded b-healthy! in New York City, pulling together a group of chefs, social justice activists, yoga teach-ers, and artists. I started writing books because I felt called to engage a diverse national audience to confront the racial, economic, and geographic differ-ences among eaters; recognize their own privileges; and reverse the negative impact the industrial food system has on our health, other animals, local economies, and the environment. In 2006, I co-authored my first book, *Grub: Ideas for an Urban Organic Kitchen*, with Anna Lappé. Three years later, my second book, *Vegan Soul Kitchen*, was published. *The Inspired Vegan* continues this dialogue.

My guiding mantra for the past ten years has been, "start with the visceral, move to the cerebral, and end the political," and I see my cookbooks as orga-nizing and base-building tools for the food justice movement. My goal is to use the sensual pleasures of the table to shift people's attitudes, habits, and politics and "eventually" ensure that everyone in this country of abun-dance—regardless of income or place of residence—has access to healthful food. Because many people are detached from having pleasurable experiences with wholesome, fresh food, I see empowering them to cook at home and share meals with family and friends as a revolutionary first step toward food justice. We can talk about local, seasonal, and sustainable for days, but if people don't feel connected to this type of food, why would they fight for it? In my mind, building community around the table and strengthening the food justice movement must go hand in hand. When you consider that educating, strategizing, and organizing for many social movements throughout the twentieth century took place in people's homes, it seems appropriate that the food revolution will find its spark in home kitchens.

main

More than just a collection of recipes, *The Inspired Vegan* assembles many of the things that excite me to live, love, laugh, lounge, and lick my fingers. Since the majority of this book was written while my wife was pregnant, our daughter was a major inspiration behind *The Inspired Vegan*'s vision. I approached it as a collage, combining my appreciation for food, design, storytelling, music, photography, and other media. To be clear, though, this is a cookbook, and my main goal is to provide you with the instructions and inspiration to prepare delicious food.

I divide the book into three parts: Basics, Interlude, and Menus. Inspired by Skye Gyngell's My Toolbox chapter in her book *A Year in My Kitchen* and David Tannis's Kitchen Rituals chapter in his book *Heart of the Artichoke and Other Kitchen Journeys*, I open *The Inspired Vegan* with Basics, where I present many of the preparation/cooking techniques and simple recipes that I find useful in my home kitchen. These nuts and bolts will strengthen your foundation for cooking and equip you with tools for improvisation and kitchen creativity. This section also provides a palette of different flavors to be used later in the Interlude and Menus sections. For example, in Basics, I share my tried-and-true Marinated Beets recipe, which transforms this underappreciated root into a delicacy virtually everyone enjoys. Later in the book, I puree these beets and use them as the base for my Bloody Sunday—a savory cocktail inspired by the Bloody Mary. The tips, ideas, and dishes in the Basics section will invite novices into a world of culinary proficiency and creativity and serve as a fresh resource for seasoned chefs.

The Interlude that follows lists the recipes included in the Menus, divided by type of dish (drinks, bites, salads, mains, sides, and sweets). I offer this bridge to give you a moment to pause, peruse, and ponder the diversity of recipes that I assemble into themed meals. This section should also be used for quick reference and inspiration for daily eating.

In the spirit of the menus created for *Grub*, I composed twelve seasonal meals for the last part of this book, inspired by family memories, social movements, personal recollections, geographic locations, unsung radical heroes, and visions for the future. For example, the Detroit Harvest menu pays homage to James and Grace Lee Boggs for their community activism in Detroit, especially the early food justice work of Detroit Summer—a youth program/collective they founded in 1992. Such dishes as the Black-Eyed Peas in Garlic-Ginger-Braised Mustard Greens with Quick-Pickled Mustard Greens, Sesame Seeds, and Tamari and Molasses, Miso, and Maple Candied Sweet Potatoes fuse elements of Afrodiasporic and Asian cuisine as a nod to the respective heritages of James and Grace Lee. While I hope these menus inspire you to bring family and friends together on weekends, days off, and holidays to collectively prepare meals and spend hours eating, connecting, and creating memories, they also serve the practical purpose of walking you through menu planning. I have heard the critique that many vegetarian and vegan cookbooks read as collections of side dishes, and people often ask me for guidance in putting together balanced menus. So I want to help you become proficient in creating satisfying meals that use whole, fresh, seasonal ingredients with beneficial proportions of fats, proteins, carbohydrates, and micronutrients. Similar to the way a stylist takes disparate pieces and puts together a stunning outfit, I have assembled dishes into mouthwatering ensembles. You have the option of making the suggested menu or mixing and matching dishes from the Interlude section for combinations that suit your schedule, tastes, and desires.

dessert

Vegetables that I grow in my home garden and food that I buy from my local farmers' market influence the recipes in this book. You should be able to find the suggested ingredients at your own farmers' market, or at a well-stocked food co-op or a supermarket. However, I encourage you to make substitutions using whatever is readily available. For example, if you are making Butter Bean and Tomato-Drenched Collards with Parsley, harvest the Lacinato kale from your home garden instead of traveling to buy collard greens. If you can't find fresh broad beans, use the chickpeas you have on hand for the Savory Grits with Sautéed Broad Beans, Roasted Fennel, and Thyme. It won't hurt my feelings if you deviate from these recipes. In fact, I want you to make them your own.

And mix dishes up, too. Combine leftover Coconut Quinoa with warm almond milk and top it with slices of Rice Wine–Poached Asian Pears with Spiced Syrup for breakfast. Stuff Funmilayo Fritters with Harissa and Purple Slaw with Toasted Pecans inside pita bread, top it with Creamy Celeriac Sauce, and wash the sandwich down with a glass of Sparkling Rosemary-Grapefruit Water. See this cookbook (and others) as a guide. In the spirit of jazz jam sessions and hip-hop ciphers, you should scat, freestyle, and let fresh seasonal ingredients, readily available staples, intuition, and your senses drive the creation of your meals. You will find that spontaneity is one of the true pleasures of cooking. Word to Guru.

If I did my job well, *The Inspired Vegan* will move seamlessly from your kitchen countertop to your coffee table to your nightstand. You will be equally informed about black and brown kids starving in the hood, animals being brutalized in factory farms, and tomato pickers being exploited in Florida. But most important, you'll be cooking.

Bryant Terry
twitter.com/bryantterry

inspiration for this book

"Adidas to Addis" by Cut Chemist
"Addis Black Widow" by Mulatu Astatke & the Heliocentrics
David Adjaye
"The African Way" & "America" by K'naan
Afro Roots by Mongo Santamaria
Angaza Africa: African Art Now
"Angola" by Cesaria Evora
Asian/American/Modern Art: Shifting Currents, 1900–1970
Jean-Michel Basquiat
"Been in the Storm So Long" by Fisk Jubilee Singers
"Black Man Time" by Lee "Scratch" Perry
Blowout Comb by Digable Planets
"Born Free" by M.I.A.
browsing Page One bookstores in Hong Kong, December 2009
"Chain Heavy" by Kanye West
Diary of an Afro Warrior by Benga
Dots and Loops by Stereolab
Elle Decoration (UK edition)
Filles de Kilimanjaro by Miles Davis
The Five Obstructions directed by Lars von Trier & Jørgen Leth
Haiku: This Other World by Richard Wright
Fred Hampton
Hank Willis Thomas: Pitch Blackness
Heart of the Artichoke and Other Kitchen Journeys by David Tannis
Jamie Magazine
Edna Lewis

Maya Lin's *Systematic Landscapes* exhibit at the DeYoung Museum, 2009

Massive Attack Concert at the Warfield in San Francisco, 5.25.10

Masters: Collage: Major Works by Leading Artists

MoMA/MoMA Bookstore

My Favourite Ingredients & *A Year in My Kitchen* by Skye Gyngell

Night Catches Us directed by Tanya Hamilton

Amara Tabor Smith and Deepwater Dance Company

SELAM: Modern Ethiopian Pop Up Kitchen

Soul Cocina / Roger Feely

http://stylenoironline.com

Heidi Swanson & 101cookbooks.com

Funmilayo Chiu Mui Terry-Koon

Alice Waters

Ida B. Wells-Barnet

basics

deepening flavors

In my opinion, flavorful stocks are indispensable in the art of making good vegan food. Obviously, they are essential as bases for tasty soups and stews, but I use stocks to enhance a wide range of dishes—from grains to gravies. For example, I use vegetable stock to add complexity to the Savory Grits with Sautéed Broad Beans, Roasted Fennel, and Thyme (page 44). I also use it as the base of the marinade in my Jerk Tempeh (page 132).

If I am making a savory recipe and it calls for water, I often use stock instead. Think of it as a building block for deepening flavor. I am not above using a boxed stock if I am pinched for time (though they typically lack the cleanness and depth of homemade stocks). But the incomparable taste of fresh stocks makes chopping vegetables and boiling them for an hour or so well worth the effort. Most often I avoid bouillon cubes to make stock, as commercial brands tend to be more salty than flavorful, especially when reduced. But I have used a no-salt vegan vegetable bouillon cube that worked fine.

good fat

Fat is a tricky thing. There is a lot of conflicting information about how much we should or should not be consuming, and it can be confusing. Some believe that we should completely avoid added fat and rely on naturally occurring fats found in whole foods. Others argue that a little extra-virgin olive oil or coconut oil is necessary for absorption of vitamins, nutrients, and phytochemicals found in fruits and vegetables. I'd suggest you do your own research to see what makes sense to you. But I will tell you this:

I eat fat. It tastes good, and I like it.

I do try to keep added fat to a minimum in my daily diet. In fact, I am fine with having very little fat throughout the week to balance the richer fare that I eat on weekends (and at restaurants). But the reality is fat helps give food that extra oomph, and my life would be a lot less exciting without it. As Linda Carucci reminds us in *Cooking School Secrets for the Real World*:

Here are a few tips when making stocks:

Use the freshest vegetables possible.

Wash everything thoroughly before boiling.

Cut vegetables into small pieces to facilitate faster breakdown.

If you want a richer (albeit sweeter) stock, roast the vegetables before simmering.

If you will be reducing the stock avoid salt, as it will become too salty when concentrated.

Although a standard vegetable stock will render great flavor within 1 hour, I often simmer mine on medium-low heat for up to 2 hours to extract even more flavor.

Stock will last for 2 to 3 days refrigerated.

Leftover stock can be frozen for a couple of months and used at a later date.

A space-saving tip for leftover stock is to freeze it in ice cube trays, then transfer the cubes to freezer bags until ready to use.

Vegetable Stock

Here I offer a simple vegetable stock that I use in a number of dishes in this book.

- 1 tablespoon extra-virgin olive oil
- 2 large onions, quartered (include skin)
- 1 large carrot, sliced thinly
- 2 celery ribs, sliced thinly
- 2 medium-size potatoes, sliced thinly
- 8 ounces button mushrooms, sliced thinly (stems included)
- 1 whole garlic bulb, unpeeled, broken up, and smashed with the back of a knife
- 2 bay leaves
- 3 sprigs fresh thyme
- ½ teaspoon coarse sea salt
- ⅛ teaspoon cayenne
- 9 cups water

In a stockpot over medium-high heat, warm the olive oil. Add the onions, carrot, celery, potatoes, mushrooms, garlic, bay leaves, thyme, salt, and cayenne and sauté, stirring often, until softened, about 5 minutes. Add the water, bring to a boil, then immediately lower the heat to medium-low. Simmer, uncovered, until the vegetables are meltingly tender, about 1 hour.

Strain the vegetables, pressing down on them to extract all their liquids. Discard (and compost) the cooked vegetables.

The Inspired Vegan

While the tongue does a good job of detecting salt, sweet, bitter, and sour, when coated with fat, the tongue becomes a hypersensitive flavor receptor. As the fat molecules coat your tongue, the chimney that is your nose aerates your mouth, and fat distributes the flavors all across the surface of your tongue, not just where your spoon deposited them.

On page 6 are recipes for two standard oils used in my kitchen. Garlic oil punches up the flavor of sautéed or roasted vegetables, and it adds zip to vinaigrettes. For example, I use garlic oil for the base of the dressing in my Wilted Dandelion Greens with Hot Garlic Dressing and Garlic Chips (page 47). No need for bacon grease here. I toss cubes of tofu and peanuts in chili oil and roast them (page 166) to yield crunchy-creamy bites. And I use chili oil for soups, stews, congee, and any other dishes that require flavorful heat. Experiment with your own combinations, using fresh and dried herbs and spices. When making infused oil, make sure to use best-quality olive oil as your base. I typically make smaller quantities and use them immediately or within 2 to 3 days. But you can store infused oils in the refrigerator for up to 1 month.

salt, fat, and acid

Vinaigrette was one of the first things I learned to make in culinary school. It is simply a mixture of oil (fat) and vinegar (acid) flavored with garlic, salt, and pepper. Mustard is usually added to stabilize the emulsion, and herbs (and sometimes spices) are often added to give it zing.

When in doubt, remember to use 1 part acid (e.g., lemon juice, balsamic vinegar, apple cider vinegar) to 3 parts fat (extra-virgin olive oil is best) plus a little bit of salt, pepper, prepared mustard, and garlic thrown in for good measure.

To yield a creamier consistency, I often use an upright blender or a hand blender for making vinaigrettes. But they can easily be whisked in a bowl. If

Garlic Oil

¾ cup extra-virgin olive oil
10 large garlic cloves, chopped finely

In a small saucepan, combine the oil and the garlic. Turn the heat to the lowest point at which the oil will simmer and cook for 30 minutes.

Strain the oil into a sterilized canning jar and let cool.

Chili Oil

4 teaspoons red pepper flakes
¼ cup peanut oil
2 tablespoons roasted sesame oil

Place the red pepper flakes in a heatproof medium-size bowl. Set aside.

In a small saucepan over medium heat, combine the oils and heat until hot but not smoking, about 2 minutes. Pour over the red pepper flakes and let cool, stirring a few times, for about 20 minutes.

dressing salad leaves, add just enough vinaigrette to coat lightly right before serving. Be sure not to overdress. Extra vinaigrette can be stored in the refrigerator for up to 3 days, but make sure you remove it for at least half an hour before adding to a salad, as dressings should always be served at room temperature.

spice it up

While there are many questions about salt and its impact on health, sea salt is one foundation for a well-stocked kitchen. In addition to bringing out the natural flavors in food, sea salt contains thirty-two minerals and trace minerals, and it aids in digestion. I always have coarse sea salt on hand for everyday cooking, and fine sea salt for baking. Pepper is essential, too, and I use whole peppercorns, grinding immediately before serving. I tend to use white pepper, as I often find black to be a bit overpowering for some dishes.

There is also a wide range of organic, fresh flavorings beyond salt and pepper that can really make your dishes pop. The spices I use most often are cayenne, cinnamon, coriander, cumin, paprika, and red pepper flakes. I'm able to grow fresh herbs such as basil, rosemary, parsley, sage, and thyme year-round. But in the event that fresh herbs aren't available I will use dried herbs. Use 1 teaspoon of dried herbs for every tablespoon of fresh ones.

Rather than purchasing premade mixes (e.g., Cajun spice mix), make your own. It will be cheaper, you will know all the spices are fresh, and you can ensure that there isn't any MSG or other unhealthy additives.

The following mixes highlight aromatic herbs and spices, and they are used in the recipes in this book. I also encourage you to play around with them to deepen the flavors of veggies, beans, or tempeh.

Here are a few suggestions for additional combinations:

Simple Balsamic: 1 part balsamic vinegar + 3 parts olive oil

Orange-Balsamic: 1 part orange juice + 1 part balsamic vinegar + 3 parts olive oil

Lemon-Thyme: 1 part lemon juice + 3 parts olive oil + minced fresh thyme

Lime-Cilantro: 1 part lime juice + 3 parts olive oil + minced fresh cilantro

Orange-Ginger: 1 part orange juice + 3 parts olive oil + minced fresh ginger

Apple Cider–Cinnamon: 1 part apple cider vinegar + 3 parts olive oil + 1 cinnamon stick (soak in the emulsion for 30 minutes, then discard)

Vinaigrette

- 2 tablespoons freshly squeezed lemon juice
- 1 tablespoon red wine vinegar
- ¾ teaspoon Dijon mustard
- 1 large garlic clove, minced
  Coarse sea salt
- ½ cup extra-virgin olive oil
  Freshly ground white pepper

In an upright blender, combine the lemon juice, vinegar, mustard, garlic, and ½ teaspoon of sea salt. Blend while slowly pouring in the oil. Wait about 5 minutes, then season with salt and pepper to taste.

Garam Masala

Garam masala is a blend of ground spices used in Indian cooking. This is a smaller quantity that can be used in a curry. If you scale up and make a larger quantity, store leftovers in a tightly sealed jar in a cool, dry place for up to 3 months or in the freezer for up to 9 months.

- ¼ teaspoon freshly ground black pepper
- ¼ teaspoon garlic powder
- ¼ teaspoon ground ginger
- ¼ teaspoon cardamom powder
- ½ teaspoon ground turmeric
- ½ teaspoon ground cumin

Harissa

This is my version of harissa, a hot chili sauce commonly eaten in North Africa. I created it as a dipping sauce for my Funmilayo Fritters, but it can be used as a condiment to spice up a range of dishes. I like heat, so I add a full tablespoon of crushed red pepper flakes. Use fewer flakes to tone down the heat.

- 3 tablespoons extra-virgin olive oil
- 1 teaspoon ground cumin
- ½ teaspoon ground coriander
- 1 tablespoon paprika
- 1 tablespoon crushed red pepper flakes
- ¼ teaspoon cayenne
- Coarse sea salt
- 1 serrano chile, seeded and minced
- 3 large garlic cloves, minced
- 2 tablespoons tomato paste
- ¼ cup plus 2 tablespoons tomato sauce
- 1 tablespoon freshly squeezed lime juice
- 2 tablespoons water
- 1 teaspoon pure maple syrup
- ¼ teaspoon freshly ground white pepper

In a saucepan over low heat, combine the olive oil, cumin, coriander, paprika, red pepper flakes, cayenne, and ½ teaspoon of salt and stir well to combine. Sauté until the mixture smells fragrant, about 3 minutes. Stir in the serrano chile and garlic and sauté for 2 more minutes. Add the tomato paste, tomato sauce, lemon juice, water, and maple syrup. Mix well, and simmer until the mixture starts to thicken, about 5 minutes.

Add the white pepper, and season with additional salt to taste. Refrigerate in a tightly sealed jar for up to 1 week.

root, squash, and roast

Tasty, nutritious, and inexpensive, root vegetables and winter squash should be a staple in your home during the colder months. In my kitchen, the easiest way to make them is to roast them in the oven. All you have to do is toss them in olive oil, transfer them to a baking sheet, and bake them at high heat. I added roasted carrots, parsnips, sweet potatoes, and yellow potatoes to my Roasted Winter Vegetable Jambalaya (page 179) to make the dish heartier and sweet, as most roasted roots caramelize as the cook. Stretch yourself by roasting beets, rutabagas, and turnips, too, and try roasting winter squashes such as acorn, butternut, delicata, and kabocha.

Here are two recipes to get you started: a mélange of roasted root vegetables and roasted butternut squash.

keep the middle

Nuts can be satisfying when eaten alone, and they contribute complexity and rich texture when added to sweet and savory dishes. Similarly, those innards that you scrape from squashes and gourds can be reserved and used in sauces and baked goods, and eaten alone as a snack.

Toasting and roasting nuts and seeds help waken them up and enhance their flavor. Most seeds scraped from winter squashes or pumpkins and separated from the stringy membrane taste pretty good when roasted, but I am partial to butternut squash seeds. Before roasting them, squeeze as much of the squash and stringy membrane from the seeds, toss them in enough olive oil to coat lightly, then cover them with a little salt mixed with your favorite blend of spices. Unless you want perfect-looking seeds for presentation, there is no need to wash them. But you can always do so in a colander and dry them with a clean towel before tossing in oil.

To get you started try these combinations:

- Cinnamon and sugar
- Paprika and cayenne

Roasted Root Vegetables

    3 pounds of your favorite peeled and diced root vegetables
    2 tablespoons extra-virgin olive oil
    ½ teaspoon coarse sea salt

Preheat the oven to 450°F.

In a large bowl, combine the vegetables, the oil, and the salt.

Transfer the vegetables to a large roasting pan and roast for 1 hour, stirring every 15 minutes for even roasting.

Roasted Butternut Squash

Although you can peel winter squash before roasting, I tend to cook with the peel on. Simply cut in half, quarters, or smaller chunks, toss in olive oil, and roast at 450°F until the flesh can easily be pierced with a knife. Remember, most varieties of winter squash can be substituted for one another in recipes.

Cajun-Creole Spice Mix

In addition to using this spice mixture for seasoning a medley of nuts (page 176), you can mix it with a basic tomato sauce to give it a New Orleans flavor or you can use it to blacken tofu.

    2 teaspoons onion powder
    1 teaspoon garlic powder
    2 teaspoons paprika
    2 teaspoons chili powder
    ¼ teaspoon cayenne
    1 teaspoon fine sea salt

- Chile and lime
- Garam Masala
- Curry powder

If a dish requires toasted seeds or nuts, I typically include directions in the recipe, but in general you can cook them in a skillet over medium-high heat for 5 to 7 minutes or toast them on a baking sheet in a 375°F oven for 15 to 20 minutes, until golden.

When purchasing nuts or seeds, buy them in small quantities, as their oils can cause them to go rancid. To extend their shelf life, store them in the freezer.

crushed herbs and nuts

Pesto is simple to make, and ingredients can be combined for endless variations. Although it is commonly used to coat pasta, it can also be used as a spread for pizza and toasted bread or as a dip for vegetables. I even enjoy it with grits (see page 107). The great thing about pesto is that it freezes extremely well. So if you want to preserve surplus herbs before they spoil, make a huge batch and freeze it in an ice cube tray before transferring to a freezer bag.

Here is a basic recipe structure that can be remixed to your tastes and desires of the moment.

pesto = fresh herbs + nuts + olive oil

From there you can add lemon juice for acid, salt for seasoning, and garlic for a little punch. And I use miso, instead of a salty cheese, to add depth. Most often, one sees pesto with basil and pine nuts. But I make it with basil + almonds; cilantro + pepitas; sage + walnuts. Sometimes I puree it until smooth. Sometimes I pulse it so the nuts have some chunkiness for texture. Sometimes I mix several herbs into one batch. It is really about experimenting and seeing what works for you. Here is a standard basil pesto, plus a quirky version that uses parsley and walnuts.

The Inspired Vegan

Basil Pesto

⅓ cup pine nuts

2 cups loosely packed fresh basil leaves

2 medium-size garlic cloves, peeled

1 tablespoon mellow white or yellow miso

¼ cup freshly squeezed lemon juice

½ cup extra-virgin olive oil

  Coarse sea salt

Preheat the oven to 350°F.

Arrange the pine nuts on a baking sheet and toast them for about 8 minutes, stirring after 4 minutes.

In the bowl of a food processor fitted with a metal blade, combine the pine nuts, basil, garlic, miso, and lemon juice and puree. Slowly add the oil and process until smooth. Add ½ teaspoon of salt.

Cover any leftover pesto with a film of olive oil in a tightly sealed jar and refrigerate for up to 2 weeks.

Parsley-Walnut Pesto

> 2 cups loosely packed fresh flat-leaf parsley leaves
> 2 medium-size garlic cloves, peeled
> 1 tablespoon mellow white or yellow miso
> ¼ cup freshly squeezed lemon juice
> Coarse sea salt
> ½ cup extra-virgin olive oil
> ⅓ cup walnuts, toasted and skins removed (page 49)

In the bowl of a food processor fitted with a metal blade, combine the parsley, garlic, miso, lemon juice, and ½ teaspoon of salt and puree. Slowly add the oil and process until smooth. Add the walnuts and pulse a few times until chunky but incorporated.

Creamed Cashews

> 1 cup raw cashews, soaked overnight and drained
> ½ cup water

In an upright blender combine the cashews and water and blend until smooth.

instead of heavy cream

Creamed cashews are another staple in my kitchen. I simply puree soaked cashews in an upright blender and use the mixture in such dishes as grits that call for creamy texture. For example, I add it to my Velvety Grits with Sautéed Summer Squash, Heirloom Tomatoes, and Parsley Walnut Pesto (page 107). I also use it in soups, smoothies, and desserts. I have experimented with other nuts, but none work as well as cashews. Be sure to use raw cashews to avoid the distinctive flavor of roasted cashews. It will last for a few days refrigerated or a few months frozen.

flavor bulbs

Caramelizing onions brings out their natural sweetness and can add nuance to a variety of recipes. For example, I use Caramelized Onion Relish (page 17) as a spread on crackers and bread. I add Roasted Garlic (page 18) to give a more buttery accent to soups, mashed potatoes, and spreads. And I add Hot Pickled Red Onions (page 16) as a garnish to creamy soups, stews, and potato dishes for a touch of acid.

clean greens

If you are reading this book, I'm assuming you already know about the immense health benefits that come along with consuming dark leafy greens such as collards, kale, spinach, and Swiss chard. You are probably already aware that they are low in calories and fat, and that they are high in dietary fiber. And I'm sure you know that they are a rich source of vitamins (including B, C, E, K, and a number of B vitamins) and minerals (e.g., calcium, iron, magnesium, and potassium).

I try to eat greens at least once per day, and I have found that cutting and cleaning them immediately after harvesting or purchasing facilitates their use when I'm ready to cook. Here is how I do it:

I like to cut them, before washing, into the size needed for a particular dish. I find that bite-size pieces are easier to work with than unwieldy, large

Hot Pickled Red Onions

¼ cup apple cider vinegar
½ cup distilled white vinegar
2 tablespoons raw organic cane sugar
¼ teaspoon red pepper flakes
Pinch of coarse sea salt
5 whole peppercorns
2 cups diced red onions

In a medium-size sauté pan over low heat, combine the vinegars, sugar, pepper flakes, salt, and peppercorns. Stir well until the sugar is completely dissolved, about 3 minutes. Add the onions, raise the heat, bring to a boil, and immediately remove from the heat. Set aside to cool.

Transfer the contents of the sauté pan to a pint-size canning jar and refrigerate until ready to use.

Caramelized Onions

Caramelizing onions is a natural way of bringing out their sweetness. You simply cook them over medium-low heat, stirring often, until they are brown and tender, about 30 minutes. As for quantities, 2 large raw onions cooked in about 1 tablespoon of olive oil will yield about 1 cup of Caramelized Onions. I've seen people add sugar to "speed up the process." Skip that, and have a little patience. You can make a big batch and keep them in the fridge until you are ready to add them to soups, stews, casseroles, dips, or whatever you'd like to punch up with some meltingly rich flavor.

Caramelized Onion Relish

 1 tablespoon extra-virgin olive oil
 1 large red onion, sliced thinly
    Coarse sea salt
 1 tablespoon raw cane sugar
 3 tablespoons red wine vinegar
 1 tablespoon water
    Freshly ground white pepper

In a small sauté pan over low heat, combine the olive oil, onion, and ¼ teaspoon of salt and sauté, stirring often, until caramelized, 10 to 12 minutes.

Stir in the sugar, red wine vinegar, and water. Raise the heat to high, and bring to a boil. Immediately lower the heat to low, and simmer until the liquid starts to thicken, about 15 minutes.

Season with white pepper to taste. Store refrigerated for up to 1 week.

Roasted Garlic

    1 large head of garlic
    3 tablespoons extra-virgin olive oil

Preheat the oven to 350°F.

Cut ¼ inch off the top of the head of garlic to expose the cloves.

Pour the oil over the garlic, and wrap in aluminum foil with the cut side facing up.

Place on a baking sheet or pan to prevent the oil from dripping into the oven, and bake until the garlic is caramelizing and tender, about 1 hour. Remove from the oven and let cool. I normally prepare Roasted Garlic immediately before using, to take advantage of its sweet creaminess.

Quick-Pickled Mustard Greens

Here is a great way to preserve surplus mustard greens and enjoy them during the off-season. Use them as a condiment to add flavor to stews, porridges, and other vegetable dishes.

1½ cups apple cider vinegar
½ cup distilled white vinegar
3 tablespoons raw organic cane sugar
¼ teaspoon salt
1 teaspoon peppercorns
2 pounds mustard greens, stems removed and sliced thinly, leaves chopped roughly (keep stems and leaves separate)
2 serrano chiles, sliced thinly

In a medium-size sauté pan over low heat, combine the vinegars, sugar, salt, and peppercorns. Stir well until the sugar is completely dissolved, about 3 minutes. Remove from the heat to let cool for a few minutes.

Meanwhile, in a large pot over high heat, bring 3 quarts of water to a boil. Add 1 tablespoon of salt. Stir in the mustard stems, and boil for 1 minute. Immediately remove from the heat, add the mustard leaves, and let sit for 1 minute. Drain in a colander, and rinse with cool water. Set aside.

Transfer the greens and stems to a large heatproof bowl or a canning jar. Add the chiles to the jar, and pour the pickling liquid over everything. Set aside.

Let pickle for at least 2 hours. If not eating immediately, transfer to the refrigerator.

leaves. If you are dealing with a smaller amount of greens, you can start with a large, clean bowl. But for larger quantities, a clean sink basin does the trick. First you add the greens, running cold water until the greens are submerged. Turn off the water and let the greens sit for a minute or so. Agitate them to help remove any soil, then lift them from the sink into a large bowl. Drain the sink of its water, and repeat until the bottom of the sink is free of any residue. Transfer the greens to a colander and drain. Obviously, if you clean delicate leaves such as lettuce, you want to dry them in a salad spinner.

power protein

Having adequate protein is key to making satisfying plant-based meals and helping you stay full for longer periods. Although most people immediately imagine tofu as the primary protein source for vegetarian and vegan diets, including tempeh and legumes are also great ways of adding heft to your meals. A few recipes in this book use tofu and tempeh and can be used as a template for making creative, flavorful dishes.

One of my favorite ways to have tofu is to oven-roast it. Sometimes I enjoy it as a dish unto itself, as I do with Tofu with Peanuts Roasted in Chili Oil (page 166). Experiment with different flavored oils, using garlic, fresh herbs, and spices. I also incorporate roasted tofu into larger dishes, as I do with Saag Tofu (page 69). I have found that roasting tempeh this way is less effective, so I sometimes slice it thinly (¼ inch thick), then panfry it in olive oil. Obviously, this method requires more fat than roasting, so I only have tempeh like this every once in a while.

Whether you use a vegetable stock, a simple marinade of tamari, or a complex barbecue sauce, cooking tofu and tempeh in a marinade (on a stovetop or in the oven) is a great way to heighten its flavor. Once they've marinated, you can bake, broil, or grill to finish them off. It is important to make sure that the sauce is thin enough to absorb the liquid, as I do with Jerk Tempeh with Cilantro Sauce (page 132). Experiment with tomato-based sauce, coconut milk curry, and pesto thinned with stock or water.

I also use tempeh to add flavor and thicken soups, sauces, and stews. Don't worry about grating it. You can simply crumble it finely and add to the liquid, as I do in my Smoky Tomatoes, Roasted Plantains, and Crumbled Tempeh (page 117).

legumes

When it comes to beans and other legumes, I tend to keep it simple. I almost always choose bulk over canned (with the exception of black beans). Whereas preparing canned beans is obviously more convenient, cooking them from scratch allows me to have control over their texture and the kind of seasonings going into them. That being said, if you are whipping up quick home-cooked meals during the week and you don't have a lot of time, it is fine to use good-quality canned beans. But I suggest starting from scratch for the recipes in this book. And if possible, opt for bulk beans over prepackaged.

You need to soak your dried beans before cooking them. But first you should spread them out on a baking sheet, sort through them, and pick out pebbles and other extraneous debris. Next, get rid of any shriveled or deformed beans. After rinsing the sorted beans a few times in cold water, place them in a pot and add enough cold water to cover them by about 2 inches, so they have room to expand. Cover the pot and store them in the refrigerator overnight. Discard any beans that float to the top. If you are in a rush, you can quick soak beans by placing them in a pot and adding enough cold water to cover them by about 2 inches, bringing them to a boil over high heat, covering the pot with a lid, and setting aside to soak for at least 1 hour.

Always drain beans of their soaking water and add fresh water to cook them. Cover your beans by 2 to 3 inches of water to ensure that they have enough room to boil (I add kombu, an edible sea vegetable, to mineralize beans and shorten their cooking time). Bring them to a boil over high heat. Lower the heat to medium and simmer for the suggested time. There are plenty of charts on the Internet with cooking times for specific beans, so refer to them if a recipe does not specify the time. Remember, the water will be evaporating as the beans are cooking, so check them every so often in case you need to add more water. And wait until the last 10 minutes of cooking before you salt your beans, otherwise you will slow down their cooking time.

go with the grain

Quick-cooking grains such as quinoa, millet, oats, grits, and rice are great for everyday meals. Quinoa and millet cook pretty quickly, usually 15 to 20 minutes. So if I am in a rush, those are my go-to grains. I eat quinoa for lunch and dinner as savory sides such as Coconut Quinoa (page 119). And I sometimes eat millet as a simple side dish or in a dessert such as Thiakry with Millet and Raisins (page 97). I enjoy them both as breakfast porridges, adding nuts and seeds, dried and fresh fruit, and rice milk and sweeteners. Sometimes I will enjoy grits as a savory dish, such as my Savory Grits with Sautéed Broad Beans, Roasted Fennel, and Thyme (page 44) or my Velvety Grits with Sautéed Summer Squash, Heirloom Tomatoes, and Parsley-Walnut Pesto (page 107).

There's more to rice than the plain old white variety; you'll notice in this book that I like to use different kinds of rice (basmati, short-grain brown, long-grain brown, black, sticky). Although most grains don't require soaking, I always soak rice overnight or a few hours before cooking, as it shortens the cooking time and makes the rice more digestible. Unlike beans that require a fresh change of water after soaking, rice can be cooked in its soaking water, so just measure out the amount of water needed for cooking, then pop it right on the stove. When cooking any grain, try not to lift the lid, as it releases steam and slows down the cooking process. And whatever you do, do not stir the grains until they're done. You will disturb the steam holes and make the grain harder to cook. And always let your grain steam for 5 to 10 minutes with the lid on when done, and then fluff with a fork.

surplus tomatoes

I always encourage people to produce food at home. The simple act of growing something—fresh herbs in a kitchen windowsill, flowers on a strip of unused soil, tomatoes in a container placed on a fire escape—is a positive step in healing our Earth and getting us in the habit of producing instead of just consuming. And it does something good for the soul.

From my experience, growing tomatoes is a great way to start honing your green thumb. Tomato plants don't require lots of space, and they typically produce an abundance of fruit. Mind you, I'm not that great of a gardener, but I can grow tomatoes.

Although my parents aren't as dedicated to year-round home gardening as my grandparents were, Mom and Dad have always kept summer plots in which they primarily grow tomatoes. So with fond childhood memories, I carry on this tradition of growing tomatoes in our home garden in Oakland.

The long growing season in the Bay Area offers us hella tomatoes to eat during the summer and fall. So in addition to making lots of tomato-based dishes and giving a good deal away, we started preserving them. I mean, let's be honest, nothing compares to a just-picked ripe tomato during the summer. But for dishes that call for them during the winter months, tomatoes that have been oven-dried, made into a sauce, or canned at home get the job done. By the way, using best-quality store-bought canned tomatoes is fine (and I certainly use them often). But opening a can of tomatoes purchased from a store cannot beat the satisfaction of opening a jar full of ones that you preserved a few months earlier.

With that in mind, I offer a recipe for oven-dried tomatoes used in White Wine–Simmered Collard Greens (page 96), one for a Basic Tomato Sauce (page 25), and one for Plum-Tomato Ketchup (page 26) that can be eaten with Bright-Black Fingerling Potatoes (page 84). These recipes are good for preserving ripe tomatoes from a local grower or your home garden and ensuring that you can enjoy the fruits of summer during months when you can only purchase tired, pale, and mealy tomatoes shipped from Mexico. *The Joy of Cooking* offers detailed instructions for canning tomatoes, and you can find some great guides online as well.

As a bonus, I include one of my favorite summer recipes that uses tomatoes—Charred Plum Tomatoes and Garlic (page 27). Perfect for summer outings.

Oven-Dried Tomatoes

These Oven-Dried Tomatoes can be used in place of store-bought sun-dried tomatoes. Use them in salads and savory dishes. Or Pureé them for dips and spreads. Because of their long cooking time, it is best to dehydrate these overnight. If possible, use enough tomatoes to fit snuggly on a parchment-lined baking sheet. But whatever you have available will work fine.

Preheat the oven to 200°F.

Cut your tomatoes in half lengthwise (or in wedges if using larger tomatoes) and place cut side up on the prepared baking sheet.

Bake until the tomatoes have shrunk and dried out, about 8 hours.

Basic Tomato Sauce

This has been my standard tomato sauce since I created it for Roasted Butternut Squash and Sage Pizzas back in 2007. I also use it for pastas and vegetable dishes that call for zing. This recipe was written for use immediately after making, but obviously it can be frozen for a later date. It usually does well frozen for up to 3 months.

3 tablespoons extra-virgin olive oil

1 teaspoon dried oregano

¼ teaspoon red pepper flakes

½ teaspoon coarse sea salt

2 large garlic cloves, minced

2 pounds ripe whole tomatoes, peeled, seeded, and coarsely chopped, or 1 (28-ounce) can whole tomatoes with their juices

½ teaspoon balsamic vinegar

In a medium-size saucepan, combine the olive oil, oregano, red pepper flakes, salt, and garlic. Raise the heat to medium-high and sauté for 1 minute, stirring frequently.

Stir in the tomatoes, raise the heat, and bring to a boil. After 30 seconds, lower the heat to medium-low and simmer for 15 minutes, stirring every few minutes. Add the balsamic vinegar, cook for an additional minute, and remove from the heat. If necessary, add additional salt.

Plum-Tomato Ketchup

  1 tablespoon extra-virgin olive oil

  ½ cup diced red onion

  ½ cup diced red bell pepper

  ¼ teaspoon paprika

  2 garlic cloves, minced

  1 cup chopped canned tomatoes

  ½ teaspoon agave nectar

  1 tablespoon red wine vinegar

  2 teaspoons tamari

  3 ripe plums, peeled, pitted, and chopped

  3 tablespoons lemon juice

     Coarse sea salt

     Freshly ground white pepper

In a large sauté pan over medium heat, combine the olive oil, onion, bell pepper, and paprika. Sauté for 8 to 10 minutes, stirring often, until starting to caramelize. Add the garlic and sauté until fragrant, about 2 minutes. Add the tomatoes, agave, vinegar, and tamari. Lower the heat to low, cover, and simmer, stirring occasionally, until thickening, about 15 minutes. Remove from the heat. Stir in the plums and lemon juice, and set aside to cool.

Transfer the ketchup to an upright blender and puree until smooth. Season with salt and pepper to taste.

Store in an airtight container in the refrigerator for up to a week.

Charred Plum Tomatoes and Garlic

    10 garlic cloves, unpeeled
     8 fresh plum tomatoes, halved lengthwise
         Extra-virgin olive oil, for drizzling
    ¼   teaspoon red pepper flakes
         Coarse sea salt
         Freshly ground white pepper
    ¼   cup minced fresh basil or thyme, for garnishing

Preheat the oven to 450°F.

Spread the garlic cloves on the bottom of a baking dish. Add the tomatoes, cut side up.

Generously drizzle the tomatoes and garlic with olive oil, and sprinkle with the red pepper flakes.

Bake until the tomatoes have softened and are charred around the edges, about 40 minutes. Season the tomatoes with salt and black pepper, and garnish with fresh herbs.

if you can't beet 'em

I hear it all the time: "I don't like beets." I understand. To be quite honest, memories of boiled-to-death and bland canned ones from childhood turned me off to beets, too, until I had them raw (who would have thought?) and learned how to marinate them. Marinating beets is so simple, and it makes the most of their unique flavor. The bonus is that beets are highly nutritious. Filled with calcium, iron, magnesium, and a number of vitamins (A, B-complex, and C), they should make a welcome addition to anyone's diet, if they aren't already. They can be especially nutritious for women, though.

When my wife got pregnant we learned that almost 80 percent of expectant mothers experience iron-deficiency anemia (about 20 percent of nonpregnant women are iron deficient). So we started researching ways to reduce her chances of developing it. Our friend Breeze suggested that we try Floradix Herbal Iron Supplement. Warm. Our friend TiTi Layo encouraged us to start mixing 1 tablespoon of pure molasses, which is high in iron, with a glass of water every day. Warmer. And then our friend Kalalea suggested beets. I pulled out my trusty copy of Rebecca Wood's *The New Whole Foods Encyclopedia* and read the following: "As their color suggests, beets are a blood tonic and so are good for anemia." Hot!

I started experimenting with all types of beet recipes. I juiced the root along with the greens in the morning. I added the root—shredded raw or marinated and cut into wedges—to salads for lunch. I sautéed the greens for dinner. I also created several recipes: Ida B. Limeade (page 142), Red Beet Tapenade (page 78), and my favorite of them all—Bloody Sunday (page 101).

Here are my recipes for Marinated Beets and Garlic-Ginger-Sautéed Beet Greens.

The Inspired Vegan

Marinated Beets

These mildly flavored beets can be eaten alone as a healthy snack, added to a salad, included as a side dish in a larger meal, or pureed and used for cocktails. If you want more intensely flavored beets: After boiling, peeling, and cutting them, toss in 2 teaspoons of olive oil and roast at 400°F for 10 minutes. Remove the beets from the oven, toss in 2 tablespoons of red wine vinegar, and roast for an additional 10 minutes. They keep in the fridge for about a week.

4 medium-size beets, scrubbed, tops and bottoms trimmed (reserve the beet greens for juicing or sautéing)

Coarse sea salt

1 tablespoon red wine vinegar

1 teaspoon raw organic cane sugar

Combine the beets, 3 quarts cold water, and 1 teaspoon salt in a medium-size pot over high heat. Boil uncovered for 25 to 30 minutes, or until the beets are easily pierced with a knife. Reserving one-quarter of the cooking water, drain the beets. Peel the beets by holding them under cold running water and rubbing their skins off with your fingers or a clean towel.

Cut the beets into your desired shape (e.g., slices, wedges, or dice).

In a medium-size bowl, combine the red wine vinegar, sugar, and the reserved cooking water. Stir well until the sugar is completely dissolved. Add the beets, toss well, cover, and refrigerate for at least 1 hour, or until ready to use.

Garlic-Ginger-Sautéed Beet Greens

The other day I had a handful of beets that a friend brought from her garden. After separating the greens from the beets, I had about ½ pound of beet greens. I removed the stems and ribs from the greens, and cut the leaves into bite-size pieces. Next, I combined 2 teaspoons of extra-virgin olive oil with ¼ teaspoon of minced fresh ginger, ¼ teaspoon of minced garlic, and a pinch of salt. I sautéed the mixture over medium heat until fragrant, and then I added the greens. I sautéed them, stirring often for about 2 minutes, added 1 teaspoon of balsamic vinegar, covered them, and cooked them for another minute.

Simple Syrup

- 2 cups raw cane sugar
- 1 cup filtered water

Combine the sugar and the water in a small saucepan over low heat. Stir well until hot to touch and the sugar is completely dissolved, about 3 minutes. Let cool and refrigerate until ready to use.

sweet life

Simple Syrup (made by combining 2 parts raw cane sugar per 1 part water) is an inexpensive way to sweeten drinks. I like combining herbs and spices with the sugar for interesting (and sometimes unusual) flavor combinations. Of course you can replace Simple Syrup with agave nectar in recipes that call for a liquid sweetener. Modify these recipes adding minced fresh herbs and ground spices to come up with endless variations.

Sugar-Cayenne Simple Syrup

2 cups raw cane sugar
1 cup filtered water
1 teaspoon cayenne

Combine the sugar and the water in a small saucepan over high heat.

Stir well until hot to touch and the sugar is completely dissolved, 3 to 5 minutes.

Set aside.

Warm a small sauté pan over medium heat. Add 1 teaspoon of cayenne, shake the pan to distribute the pepper in an even layer, and cook for 10 seconds. Remove the pan from the heat, continuing to shake for 10 seconds. Repeat this step two more times. It might help to turn away from the stove as you are shaking the pan to avoid the strong cayenne smell getting into your eyes and nose.

Return the pan to the heat, immediately add the Simple Syrup, and bring to a simmer. Lower the heat to low and cook for 2 minutes, stirring occasionally. Set aside, and let cool for 1 hour.

Store in an airtight container in the refrigerator for up to 1 month.

interlude

drinks

ℚ

ambrosia punch, 102

bissap cooler, 90

bloody sunday, 101

cherry sangria, 77

chrysanthemum tea, 159

cinnamon-tamarind agua fresca , 116

fiery ginger beer / black star lime, 128

ida b. limeade, 142

kumquat-tangerine-meyer lemonade, 163

masala chai, 65

meyer sipping gingerly
(my, you're sipping gingerly), 153

minted citrus sweet tea, 53

ronald dorris , 175

slurricane shooter, 173

sour orange daiquiri, 174

sparkling rosemary-grapefruit water, 42

strawberry-basil agua fresca, 115

bites

ℚ

cajun-creole-spiced mixed nuts, 176

paprika peanuts, 43

red beet tapenade crostini, 78

toasted cashews, 159

salads

ℚ

crunchy chopped salad with creamy herb dressing, 103

purple slaw with toasted pecans, 135

simple salad of butter lettuce and fresh
spring herbs with meyer lemon vinaigrette, 54

sliced cucumber and mint salad, 91

mains
☙

2-rice congee with steamed spinach
and other accompaniments, 164

afro-asian jung with
shoyu-vinegar-chili sauce, 154

aromatic asparagus and sweet
potato curry with cilantro, 67

black-eyed peas in garlic-ginger-braised
mustard greens with quick-pickled mustard greens,
sesame seeds, and tamari, 143

butter bean and tomato-drenched
collards with parsley, 57

creamy chard soup with tostones, 130

funmilayo fritters with harissa, 92

gumbo zav, 177

jerk tempeh with cilantro sauce, 132

open-faced grilled eggplant, red onion,
and heirloom tomato sandwiches
with creamy celeriac sauce, 81

roasted winter vegetable jambalaya, 179

savory grits with sautéed broad beans,
roasted fennel, and thyme, 44

smoky tomatoes, roasted plantains,
and crumbled tempeh, 117

strawberry gazpacho shooters
with crispy rosemary, 79

tofu with peanuts roasted in chili oil, 166

tortillas stuffed with swiss chard,
currants, and spicy guacamole, 120

velvety grits with sautéed summer squash,
heirloom tomatoes, and parsley-walnut pesto, 107

sides
☙

black "forbidden" rice with parsley, 145

bright-black fingerling potatoes with
fresh plum-tomato ketchup, 84

coconut quinoa, 119

double garlic rice, 134

garlic-braised gai laan (chinese broccoli), 158

molasses, miso, and maple
candied sweet potatoes, 146

quick-pickled mustard greens, 19

red beans with thick gravy
and roasted garlic, 181

rustic johnny cakes with
caramelized onion relish, 55

saag tofu, 69

sweet potato–cornmeal drop
biscuits with maple syrup, 105

wet jollof rice with carrots, cabbage,
and parsley-garlic paste, 94

white wine–simmered collard greens
with oven-dried tomatoes, 96

wilted dandelion greens with hot garlic
dressing and garlic chips, 47

yellow basmati rice, 71

sweets

Ç

café brûlot lace cookies, 183

cardamom-saffron sweet lassi
with candied cashews, 72

chewy lemon-coconut cookies with lemon icing, 60

citrus-hibiscus sorbet, 137

frozen café no lait with
nutmeg and chocolate shavings, 110

ginger-molasses cake with
molasses-coated walnuts, 48

gingered black sesame-seed brittle, 168

mexican chocolate pudding
and agave-coated pepitas, 123

raspberry-lime ice pops, 86

rice wine–poached asian
pears with spiced syrup, 148

thiakry with millet and raisins, 97

menus

grits. greens. molasses.

Ϙ

sparkling rosemary-grapefruit water
paprika peanuts
savory grits with sautéed broad beans, roasted fennel, and thyme
wilted dandelion greens with hot garlic dressing and garlic chips
ginger-molasses cake with molasses-coated walnuts

SOUNDTRACK

Chicago: The Living Legends—Lil Hardin Armstrong and Her Orchestra
Complete Atomic Basie by Count Basie
Jazz Party by Duke Ellington
The Complete Billie Holiday
The Father of Stride Jazz by James Price Johnson

Whenever I go back to visit my sisters and brothers, we relive old times, remembering the past. And when we share again in gathering wild strawberries, canning, rendering lard, finding walnuts, picking persimmons, making fruitcake, I realize how much the bond that held us had to do with food.

—EDNA LEWIS

Although I had intended to start this section with a meal that highlights food of the African diaspora, the idea for this particular menu came about rather arbitrarily. I had just returned from a weeklong visit with my parents in Huntsville, Alabama, for the end-of-year holidays. My intentions of eating lightly and running every morning while there did not come to fruition. Instead, though I am somewhat embarrassed to admit it, I pigged out and slept in every day. Each moment was precious, though, as I also spent a lot of time reconnecting with Mom and Dad—cooking, eating Mom's food, hiking, bowling (on Wii), and sitting next to them watching their favorite television shows, creating new family memories.

I returned home determined to jump back into my exercise ritual of powering through a five AM spin class followed by an hour-long heart-pounding boot camp class. But that Monday morning I paid for my week of excess and inactivity. As I hunched over, panting after running up a steep hill, two of my fellow boot campers—TiTi Layo and Al—teased me about being out of shape. "I'm full of grits, greens, and molasses," I blurted. "That sounds like the name of a menu you should create," Al replied.

When I returned home from my workout, I reflected upon my interaction with Al and TiTi Layo. I wondered why I uttered "grits, greens, and molasses" (particularly as I had not eaten any of those foods during my trip). I wasn't trying to be cute. It was involuntary, like belching after scarfing down a meal. In fact, that early in the morning, I'm still operating from my reptilian brain, so I concluded that there was something subconscious operating in the moment. I then realized that my response was connected to memories of my childhood.

Somewhere deep within me, grits, greens, and molasses—those three ingredients that Ma'Dear (my maternal grandmother) used to cook with so often when I spent carefree summers with her as a kid—had become a metaphor for the comfort and happiness of spending time with my family. So it was more than just grits, greens, and molasses that influenced these recipes. I also drew inspiration from memories of growing up in a family that bonded over comforting, home-cooked meals as well as the collective history of African Americans using local, seasonal, and wholesome food.

I also think it is important that these recipes further chip away at the deep-fried stereotypes of "soul food." As I often remind people, I am simply celebrating the type of fare that my ancestors enjoyed. The food that my grandparents ate on a daily basis was as local as their backyard garden; they always ate in season (except for food they preserved); my paternal grandfather proudly proclaimed that he had a "natural" (read: no chemical pesticides) garden; and when my maternal grandmother spent all Saturday cooking a meal for the following day, that was the slowest of food.

Don't get me wrong—while I think it's unfortunate that comfort foods such as fried chicken, red velvet cake, and macaroni and cheese tend to hog all the attention in the popular imagination, I certainly don't think we should discard or ignore the fatty-sugary foods of African American cuisine. I like to indulge every once in a while, just as much as the next person. I simply want to challenge people to move beyond obvious ingredients and dishes and discover the hidden narrative of African American cooking.

I want us all to learn more about—and appreciate—the diverse ingredients, regional variations, modern interpretations, and complexity of this deeply rooted cuisine.

www.southernfoodways.com

YIELD
4 servings

SOUNDTRACK
"Ice Man" by Memphis Minnie from
*Memphis Minnie—Complete
Recorded Works, Vol. 2*

FILM
Soul Food Junkies directed by Byron
Hurt

Sparkling Rosemary-Grapefruit Water

With rosemary-infused simple syrup and freshly squeezed grapefruit juice, this light and refreshing drink has a perfumy essence—a perfect complement to a breezy spring afternoon. While I suggest enjoying this drink with ice, you can always have it at room temperature. I would simply add more sparkling water to taste, as the flavor is concentrated. The rosemary-infused simple syrup can also be used in lemonades and other drinks that would benefit from added sweetener.

- ¼ cup filtered water
- ½ cup raw cane sugar
- ¼ cup rosemary, rough chopped
- 1 cup freshly squeezed ruby red grapefruit juice with pulp (about two large grapefruits)
- 5 cups chilled sparkling water
- 4 (3- to 4-inch) rosemary sprigs, for garnishing

Make a simple syrup by combining the filtered water, sugar, and chopped rosemary in a small saucepan over high heat. Stir well, occasionally, until hot to the touch and the sugar is completely dissolved, about 3 minutes. Remove from the heat and set aside to allow the rosemary flavor to infuse for at least 30 minutes.

Strain the simple syrup into a serving pitcher, pressing the rosemary against the sieve to extract all the liquid, and compost the chopped rosemary. Add the grapefruit juice and stir well to combine. Just before serving, add the sparkling water and stir gently to combine.

Ladle into pint-size canning jars filled with ice cubes and garnish each serving with a whole rosemary sprig.

Paprika Peanuts

Paprika gives these peanuts a tempting reddish-orange tint and a mildly smoky-sweet taste that is subtly flavorful and not overpowering. They can be filling, so try not to overload on them before a meal. Like all spices, paprika should be as fresh as possible to get the most flavor from it. So just give it a whiff to check.

YIELD
4 cups

SOUNDTRACK
"Salt Peanuts" by the Pointer Sisters from *The Pointer Sisters: Yes We Can Can—The Best of the Blue Thumb Recordings*

BOOK
The Man Who Talks with the Flowers: The Intimate Life Story of Dr. George Washington Carver by Glenn Clark

- 4 cups raw shelled peanuts (without skins)
- 2 tablespoons paprika
- ¼ teaspoon cayenne
- 1 teaspoon raw organic cane sugar
- 1 teaspoon fine sea salt
- 3 tablespoons peanut or light olive oil

Preheat the oven to 350°F.

Spread the peanuts in an even layer on a parchment-lined baking sheet. Bake, stirring every 5 minutes to ensure even roasting, until the peanuts start to become crisp and fragrant, about 20 minutes.

While the peanuts are roasting, combine the paprika, cayenne, sugar, and salt in a small bowl and mix well to combine. Set aside.

Pour the peanut oil into a large mixing bowl. Transfer the roasted peanuts to the bowl and stir well to coat the peanuts completely. Add the spice blend to the bowl and stir well to coat. Transfer the peanuts back to the baking sheet and roast for 5 more minutes.

Remove from the oven and cool for at least 15 minutes before serving.

Store any leftovers in an airtight container in the refrigerator.

YIELD
4 to 6 servings

SOUNDTRACK
"Walkin Blues'" by Robert Johnson
from *Robert Johnson—The Complete
Recordings*

BOOK
*Hammer and Hoe: Alabama
Communists During the Great
Depression* by Robin D. G. Kelley

Savory Grits with Sautéed Broad Beans, Roasted Fennel, and Thyme

Warm, creamy, and scrumptious, this dish will become a standard comfort food in your family's home. The broad beans (also known as fava beans) give it an earthy richness, and the soft, melting texture of the roasted fennel adds subtle complexity. If they are available, use spring-fresh broad beans. Otherwise frozen fava beans, which you'll find at most Middle Eastern markets, will work fine for this recipe. If broad beans are not available, fresh or frozen lima beans are a good substitution. And please make sure you use grits (I prefer yellow), not polenta, their close cousin. By the way, the roasted fennel is great as a stand-alone side dish.

Fennel

- 2 medium-size fennel bulbs (about ¾ pound each)
  Freshly ground black pepper
- 2 teaspoons extra-virgin olive oil
- ¼ teaspoon coarse sea salt

Broad Beans

- A little over 2 pounds of fresh broad beans, or 2 cups frozen broad beans, thawed
- 2 teaspoons extra-virgin olive oil
- 1 large garlic clove, minced
- ½ cup Vegetable Stock (page 4)
- ½ teaspoon coarse sea salt
- 1 tablespoon fresh thyme

Grits

2 tablespoons extra-virgin olive oil, and more for drizzling if you like

¼ cup finely chopped onions

1 teaspoon ground cumin

Coarse sea salt

4 cups Vegetable Stock (page 4)

¾ cup yellow grits

½ cup Creamed Cashews (page 14)

Freshly ground white pepper

For the fennel

Preheat the oven to 375°F.

Cut the stalks and fronds off the fennel, so you are left with just the round white bulbs at the base. Cut each bulb, lengthwise, into eight pieces and remove the core.

In a large bowl, combine the olive oil with the salt. Add the fennel and toss well to coat.

Arrange the fennel on a parchment-lined baking sheet and roast until the fennel begins to caramelize, about 40 minutes, stirring every 10 minutes for even roasting.

Sprinkle with pepper and set aside.

For the beans

If using fresh broad beans, shell, blanch, and peel them, then set them aside (see sidebar). If using frozen beans, rinse them until they are thawed and set them aside to drain.

Shelling, Blanching, and Peeling Fresh Broad Beans

First, bend the tip of the tough outer shell, pull down the seam, and remove the bean inside. In a saucepan over high heat, bring water to a boil. Add the broad beans and cook for about 45 seconds. Drain and immediately rinse in cold running water. Transfer the beans to a bowl filled with cold water. Pinch each bean to remove its skin. Discard the skin.

Combine the olive oil and garlic in a large skillet over medium heat and sauté until fragrant and golden, about 2 minutes. Add the stock, the salt, and the reserved beans. Lower the heat to medium-low, partially cover the skillet, and simmer until the beans are tender, 12 to 14 minutes. Add the thyme, stir the mixture well, and cook for an additional minute.

For the grits

In a medium-size sauté pan over medium heat, warm 2 tablespoons of the olive oil and add the onion, cumin, and ½ teaspoon of salt. Cook for about 7 minutes, stirring occasionally, until softened. Set aside.

In a medium-size saucepan, combine 3 cups of the stock and ½ teaspoon of salt and bring to a boil. Whisk the grits into the liquid until no lumps remain. Return to a boil, then quickly lower the heat to low. Simmer, whisking occasionally to prevent the grits from sticking to the bottom of the pan, until the grits have absorbed most of the liquid and are beginning to thicken, 3 to 5 minutes. Add the remaining cup of stock and simmer for another 10 minutes, whisking occasionally, until most of the liquid has been absorbed. Stir in the ½ cup of Creamed Cashews and the onion mixture, cover, and simmer, whisking frequently, until the grits are soft and fluffy, about 30 minutes.

If desired, add a few tablespoons of water to thin out the grits.

Season with salt and white pepper to taste.

Top each serving of grits with several slices of roasted fennel and about ½ cup of the beans. If desired, drizzle each serving with a little olive oil.

Wilted Dandelion Greens with Hot Garlic Dressing and Garlic Chips

This is my remix of Wilted Dandelion Greens with Hot Bacon Dressing found in Jessica B. Harris's The Welcome Table: African-American Heritage Cooking. *If dandelion greens are not available, use Swiss chard that has been stemmed and cut into bite-size pieces.*

1 pound dandelion greens, torn into bite-size pieces

1 tablespoon extra-virgin olive oil

5 large cloves garlic, sliced thinly

1 teaspoon raw organic cane sugar, or ½ teaspoon agave nectar

¼ teaspoon coarse sea salt

2 tablespoons apple cider vinegar

Wash the greens well, drain them in a colander, and dry them in a salad spinner (or pat them dry with a clean kitchen towel). Place the greens in a large serving bowl and set aside.

In a small skillet, combine the oil and garlic. Turn the heat on low and simmer until the garlic is crispy and golden brown, 5 to 7 minutes. With a fork, transfer the garlic to the serving bowl with the greens. After all the garlic is removed, raise the heat to high and quickly add the sugar, salt, and apple cider vinegar to the skillet. Stir until the sugar has dissolved, about 3 minutes. After the sugar has dissolved, heat the vinaigrette without disturbing for 30 seconds or so, then immediately pour the dressing over the greens. With a fork or tongs, quickly toss to combine, and serve immediately.

YIELD
4 to 6 servings

SOUNDTRACK
Bessemer Bound Blues by Ma Rainey from *Ma Rainey*

BOOKS
Making a New Deal: Industrial Workers in Chicago, 1919–1939 by Lizabeth Cohen

The Jungle by Upton Sinclair

YIELD
6 to 8 servings

SOUNDTRACK
"There Is No Greater Love" by Dinah
Washington from *Ultimate: Dinah
Washington*

BOOK
*Moses: When Harriet Tubman Led Her
People to Freedom* by Carole Boston
Weatherford with illustrations by
Kadir Nelson

Ginger-Molasses Cake with Molasses-Coated Walnuts

This cake is rich, full of flavor, and unbelievably moist. It reminds me of times spent gliding back and forth on the rusty metal bench rocker on my grandmother's porch. I coat the walnuts with molasses to add another layer of flavor with every bite. While you only need ¾ cup of the walnuts for the cake, I suggest making 2 cups so you can eat them as a prelude to the meal, along with the cake, or as a snack later on. If you can't find walnuts with the skin already removed, you will need to remove the skin to avoid its bitterness.

Molasses-Coated Walnuts

2 cups raw walnut halves, toasted and skins removed (see note)

1 tablespoon light olive oil

2 tablespoons molasses

2 tablespoons raw cane sugar

¼ teaspoon fine sea salt

Ginger-Molasses Cake

½ cup whole wheat pastry flour

1 cup all-purpose flour

1 teaspoon baking soda

1 tablespoon plus 1 teaspoon ground ginger

½ teaspoon fine sea salt

½ cup plus 2 tablespoons maple sugar or raw cane sugar

1 cup unflavored rice milk

½ cup plus 1 tablespoon molasses

6 tablespoons coconut oil

1 tablespoon apple cider vinegar

¾ cup roughly chopped molasses-coated walnuts
Confectioners' sugar, for dusting

For the walnuts

In a large mixing bowl, combine the walnuts with the olive oil and stir until the walnuts are thoroughly coated. Add the molasses and stir until thoroughly coated, then add the sugar and salt and stir until thoroughly coated.

Warm a large, heavy cast-iron skillet over medium-high heat, about 3 minutes. Place the walnuts in the skillet, scraping the bowl with a rubber spatula to remove every drop of the molasses mixture, and stir constantly until the walnuts are fragrant, about 1½ minutes.

Transfer the walnuts to a sheet of parchment paper and quickly spread out, separating them with two forks. Set aside to cool.

For the cake

Preheat the oven to 350°F. Oil and flour a 9-inch loaf pan.

Sift the flours, baking soda, ginger, and salt into a large bowl. Add the sugar, and whisk together until well blended.

In a medium-size bowl, combine the rice milk, molasses, coconut oil, and apple cider vinegar and vigorously whisk until well blended.

Immediately add the wet ingredients to the dry ingredients, and stir until just combined (a few small lumps are fine).

Fold the molasses-coated walnuts into the batter.

Pour the batter into the prepared pan, scraping out all the contents, and spread evenly.

Bake for 40 to 50 minutes, until a toothpick inserted in the center comes out clean. Serve warm dusted with confectioners' sugar.

Toasting Walnuts and Removing Their Skins

While naturally sweet in flavor, walnuts have a bitter outer skin, which you will want to remove. First, preheat the oven to 350°F. Spread the walnuts on a parchment paper–lined baking sheet and toast for 8 minutes, stirring at the 4-minute point. Remove from the oven and set aside until the walnuts are cool enough to touch. Transfer the walnuts to a sieve and, holding the sieve over the sink, rub the walnuts against the wire until the skins loosen and fall off. Set aside to completely cool. Although you will get the freshest most flavorful walnuts by purchasing them in the shell and cracking them just before you use them, this process can be time consuming. So I buy shelled, walnut halves and store them in the freezer to extend their freshness.

freedom fare

Q

minted citrus sweet tea

simple salad of butter lettuce and
fresh spring herbs with meyer lemon vinaigrette

rustic johnny cakes with caramelized onion relish

butter bean and tomato-drenched collards with parsley

chewy lemon-coconut cookies with lemon icing

SOUNDTRACK

What If I Am a Woman?, Volumes 1 and 2: Black Women's Speeches
narrated by Ruby Dee with an introduction by Ossie Davis

The Times They Are A-Changin' by Bob Dylan

The Revolution Will Not Be Televised by Gil Scott-Heron

Odetta Sings Ballads and Blues by Odetta

Protest Anthology by Nina Simone

Radical simply means grasping things at the root.

—ANGELA DAVIS

The idea for this menu came after my friend Brett Cook gifted his 16" x 20" line drawing inspired by the Free Breakfast for Children Program, which was one of the major sources of inspiration for my work as a food justice activist.

Started by the Black Panther Party in 1969 with the help of the pastor of St. Augustine's Church in West Oakland, California, this project served food to poor children living in the Bay Area and addressed issues of poverty, malnutrition, and institutional racism/classism in one fell swoop. The Panthers were clear that for historically oppressed communities to be free they had to be well fed, and the pilot program was so successful they replicated it in major cities across the United States. Within one year, the organization was feeding over ten thousand young people every morning before school.

While doing research on this program in graduate school and interviewing former Black Panthers about its origin, I better understood the connection between food access in low-income neighborhoods and chronic illnesses. I was moved to play a part in creating healthier communities. So in 2001, I enrolled in culinary school and started offering pro bono cooking classes to youth throughout New York City. That same year, with a desire to marry the sensual pleasures of the table with social justice activism, I founded b-healthy!—an initiative that used cooking to empower young people to become active in the movement to create a healthy, just, and sustainable food system.

This menu is a nod to the cutting-edge and inspirational "survival programs" run by the Panthers in the late 1960s and '70s. And these dishes also pay homage to the millions of African Americans who migrated from the South to West Coast cities such as Los Angeles, Long Beach, and Oakland during the Second Great Migration. I imagine that those recent transplants, like me, found comfort in re-creating familiar dishes in their new geographical context.

You shouldn't have to travel far to gather the elements needed to make these recipes, as most can be prepared using standard ingredients from a well-stocked pantry and a basic home garden. Eaten together, these dishes make a satisfying light meal. To add heft to this meal, add a whole grain rice or barley.

growingpower.org • *mxgm.org* • *peoplesgrocery.org*

Minted Citrus Sweet Tea

This tea is best enjoyed over ice on a warm afternoon. The large quantity should leave you with enough for a few days, but make sure you remove any citrus fruits before refrigerating overnight to avoid bitterness. As with most drinks to be served over ice, I made this one slightly sweeter in anticipation of melting ice.

YIELD
About 1 gallon

SOUNDTRACK
"Mississippi Goddamn" by Nina Simone from *Protest Anthology*

BOOK
Angela Davis: An Autobiography

2 cups raw cane sugar, or 1½ cups agave nectar

12 cups cold water

1 cup loosely packed fresh mint leaves

10 orange pekoe tea bags

1½ cups fresh orange juice

1 cup fresh lemon juice

Ice cubes

Thin lemon slices, for garnish

Fresh mint leaves, for garnish

Make a minted simple syrup by combining the sugar, 1 cup of the water, and the mint leaves in a small saucepan over high heat. Stir well until hot to touch and the sugar is completely dissolved, about 3 minutes. Remove from the heat and set aside to cool.

In a large saucepan over high heat, bring the remaining 11 cups of water to a boil. Remove from the heat and immediately add the tea bags. Cover and steep for 30 minutes.

Take off the lid and remove the tea bags with a slotted spoon, pressing the bags on the side of the saucepan to release their liquids. Strain the mint leaves from the simple syrup and discard. Stir in the orange juice, lemon juice, and 1½ cups of the simple syrup, or more to taste, and allow the tea to cool.

Ladle into pint-size canning jars filled with ice cubes and garnish with lemon slices plus fresh mint leaves.

YIELD
4 to 6 servings

SOUNDTRACK
"Supermarket Blues" by Eugene
McDaniels from *Headless Heroes of
the Apocalypse*

BOOK
Assata: An Autobiography

Simple Salad of Butter Lettuce and Fresh Spring Herbs with Meyer Lemon Vinaigrette

Sometimes a simple salad that uses the freshest seasonal lettuces and herbs is all one needs to precede a flavorful meal. A simple vinaigrette with lemon as its acid is best for highlighting the spring's offerings. For this dressing, simply use Meyer lemons in the recipe for Vinaigrette (page 8).

2   heads butter lettuce, torn into bite-size pieces
1   cup mixed fresh herb leaves such as basil, chervil, dill, mint, parsley, sage, tarragon, or oregano
    Vinaigrette (page 8)

In a large salad bowl, combine the lettuce with the herbs.

Toss with just enough Vinaigrette to coat lightly.

Rustic Johnny Cakes with Caramelized Onion Relish

Although slathering Caramelized Onion Relish does liven up the flavor of these flat cornmeal cakes, I must admit I am partial to eating them after they have soaked in the tangy tomato broth of Butter Bean and Tomato-Drenched Collards (page 57). I simply add a few dollops of onion relish to the soup for more zing. These cakes are also great with pure maple syrup or jam for breakfast.

YIELD
12 cakes

SOUNDTRACK
"Soul Power" by James Brown from *Funk Power 1970—A Brand New Thang*

BOOK
Soledad Brother: The Prison Letters of George Jackson

1½ cups stone-ground cornmeal

½ cup whole wheat pastry flour

1 teaspoon baking powder

1 teaspoon fine sea salt

2¼ cups unflavored rice milk

Coconut oil, for frying

Caramelized Onion Relish (page 17)

In a large bowl, combine the cornmeal, flour, baking powder, and salt. Set aside.

In a small saucepan, bring the rice milk to a boil, then slowly pour over the cornmeal mixture, stirring as you pour. Mix well, and refrigerate the batter for 30 minutes.

While the batter is resting in the refrigerator, preheat the oven to 250°F.

Warm a large, nonstick skillet or a well-oiled griddle over medium-high heat, and grease well with 1 tablespoon of coconut oil. Add ¼ cup of batter to the skillet per cake. A large skillet should comfortably fit two to three. After about 1 minute, when the bottom starts to set, lower the heat to medium-low. Use a wooden spoon to shape the cakes, pushing them in and up while they are cooking. The cakes don't have to be perfect; they simply should not be spreading all over the place. Cook for 4 to 6 minutes per side, adding more oil after turning, until they are golden brown and crispy on the outside (do this in several batches). Transfer the cooked cakes from the skillet to a baking sheet and then hold them in the oven until all the cakes are cooked.

Serve with Caramelized Onion Relish.

Butter Bean and Tomato-Drenched Collards with Parsley

This rich, deep, and full-flavored stew was inspired by the Braised Lacinato Kale with Tomato and Anchovy Soffritto recipe from the cookbook A16: Food + Wine. The creamy texture and delicate flavor of butter beans, also known as lima beans, complement the tomato broth well. I prefer dried beans for this recipe, but you can use fresh butter beans if they are in season (frozen will work, too). As with most soups and stews, the taste of this one is off the charts after the flavors have married for a few hours or overnight.

YIELD
4 to 6 servings

SOUNDTRACK
"The Times They Are a-Changin'" by Odetta from *Odetta Sings Dylan*

BOOK
Body and Soul: The Black Panther Party and the Fight Against Medical Discrimination by Alondra Nelson

The Hood Health Handbook edited by C'BS Alfie Allah and Supreme Understanding

Beans

1½   cup dried butterbeans, sorted, soaked overnight, drained, and rinsed

1   (3-inch) piece kombu
     Coarse sea salt

Collards

1   packed cup oven- or sun-dried tomatoes

2   pounds collards (about 2 large bunches), ribs removed and sliced thinly, leaves cut into bite-size pieces (keep them separate)
    Coarse sea salt

1   tablespoon freshly squeezed lemon juice

2   tablespoons red wine vinegar

2   tablespoons tomato paste

3   tablespoons extra-virgin olive oil

1   medium-size yellow onion, diced finely

4   garlic cloves, minced

1   serrano chile, sliced thinly

5½   cups vegetable stock (page 4)

¼   cup minced fresh parsley

For the beans

In a medium-size saucepan over medium heat, combine the butter beans with the kombu and enough water to cover them by 2 inches. Bring to a boil. Lower the heat to medium-low and simmer, partially covered, until the beans are just tender, 25 to 45 minutes depending on their age. You want the beans to be firm, so watch them closely to ensure they do not start falling apart. When they seem to be close to done, add 1 teaspoon of salt, *gently* stir, and simmer for another 5 minutes. Be sure to skim off any floating bean skins and foam while the beans are cooking.

Drain the beans, rinse them in cold water for 1 minute or so, and set aside to cool. Remove the kombu and compost it.

For the collards

Place the tomatoes in a small bowl, add enough boiling water to cover, and set aside for 20 minutes.

Next, rinse and drain the collard stems and leaves (keeping them separate).

In a large pot over high heat, bring 3 quarts of water to a boil and add 1 tablespoon of salt. Add the collard stems and cook, uncovered, for 2 minutes. Add the leaves and cook until softened, 2 to 3 minutes. Remove from the heat, drain, rinse, and set aside.

Drain the tomatoes, reserving their liquid, and transfer them to an upright blender.

Add the lemon juice, red wine vinegar, tomato paste, and 1 cup of the reserved tomato liquid to the blender and blend until creamy. Set aside.

In the large pot used above, over medium heat, combine the olive oil, onion, and ½ teaspoon of salt. Sauté until the onion is soft, about 5 minutes. Add the garlic and chile and sauté until fragrant and turning golden, about 3 minutes. Add the tomato mixture, cover, and simmer over low heat for about 20 minutes, until the puree starts to thicken. Stir frequently.

Add the reserved collard leaves and stems, the vegetable stock, and the reserved beans. Stir well, partially cover, and simmer on low heat for 30 minutes, until the greens are meltingly tender. Add the parsley, cook for an additional minute, and season with pepper and additional salt if necessary.

YIELD
 About 2 dozen 2½-inch cookies

SOUNDTRACK
 "Hello Sunshine" by Aretha Franklin
 from *Aretha Now*

BOOK
 Lemons Are Not Red by Laura Vaccaro
 Seeger

Chewy Lemon-Coconut Cookies with Lemon Icing

With a cup of hot herbal tea, these lemony cookies brighten up dreary afternoons. Eaten plain they are flavorful, but topped with lemon icing they are next level.

Icing

- 2 cups confectioners' sugar, sifted
- 3 tablespoons freshly squeezed lemon juice
- 1 tablespoon water
- 1 teaspoon lemon zest

Cookies

- 1 heaping tablespoon ground flaxseeds (whole flaxseeds will not do)
- 3 tablespoons water
- ½ cup solidified coconut oil (a.k.a. coconut butter)
- ¾ cup raw cane sugar
- 1 tablespoon lemon zest
- 3 tablespoons freshly squeezed lemon juice
- ½ cup plus 3 tablespoons all-purpose flour
- ½ cup whole wheat pastry flour
- 1 cup shredded unsweetened coconut
- ½ teaspoon baking soda
- ¼ teaspoon fine sea salt

For the icing

In a medium-size bowl, stir together the sugar, lemon juice, water, and lemon zest until smooth.

For the cookies

In an upright blender, combine the flaxseed powder and water and blend until creamy. Pour the mixture into a large bowl and add the solidified coconut oil, sugar, lemon zest, and lemon juice. Beat with a spoon until well blended, and set aside.

In a medium-size mixing bowl, whisk together the flours, ½ cup of the coconut, and the baking soda and salt.

Combine the dry mixture with the wet mixture and stir just until well combined and smooth in texture.

Cover and refrigerate the batter for at least 30 minutes before baking.

Preheat the oven to 350°F.

Drop the dough by tablespoons, about 2 inches apart, onto two parchment-lined or well-greased baking sheets. Bake until the edges are starting to turn golden, 10 to 12 minutes, rotating the sheets halfway through the baking time. Let cool for 2 minutes on the sheets, then transfer the cookies to a wire rack to let cool completely.

Spread the cookies with lemon icing. Sprinkle each cookie with ½ to 1 teaspoon of the remaining coconut and let set for about 1 hour.

south asian supper

♀

masala chai

aromatic asparagus and sweet potato curry with cilantro

saag tofu

yellow basmati rice

cardamom-saffron sweet lassi with candied cashews

SOUNDTRACK

A History of Now by Asian Dub Foundation

Hello Hello by MIDIval Punditz

The Essential Ravi Shankar

An Exquisite Raag in a Live Concert
by Shivkumar Sharma and Zakir Hussain

It Takes a Thief by Thievery Corporation

If there's nothing that's lovely, and if there's nothing that's
just ephemeral, that you can just lie on the floor and bust
a gut laughing at, then what's the point?

—ARUNDHATI ROY

To start, I must make two things clear: (1) I refuse, no matter what the cir-
cumstance, to eat asparagus out of season. (2) I feel negligent in my duties
as a chef if I do not take full advantage of asparagus when it arrives at farmers'
markets in spring. As far as I'm concerned, in-season asparagus is best enjoyed prepared simply. So I typically bring a pot of generously salted water
to a boil, remove it from the heat, add trimmed asparagus for 1 minute or so,
drain the asparagus, toss it in extra-virgin olive oil, and dust it with fine sea
salt and freshly ground white pepper. That's it. Al dente, mildly seasoned,
and deeply flavorful.

A few years ago, I was asked to contribute recipes to a green sex guide
called *Eco-Sex*. The idea was that I would compose a menu for an imaginary

date with a smokin' hot woman, using ingredients that increase erotic desire and enhance performance. I requested that the author of the book, Stefanie Weiss, e-mail a list of aphrodisiacs gleaned from her extensive research. She sent the following:

Foods: papaya, pine nuts, soy, chocolate, *asparagus*, almond, avocado, basil, fennel, figs, goji berries, truffles, artichokes, *ginger*

Herbs: licorice, *saffron*, durian, passion flower, damiana, shatavari, angelica

Arginine rich foods (an important amino acid for a man's sexual performance): granola, oatmeal, peanuts, *cashews*, walnuts, *green vegetables*, *root vegetables*, *garlic*, ginseng, *coconut milk*, soybeans

It was late March, and asparagus was at its peak in Northern California. So, naturally, I had to incorporate those tender shoots into my seductive meal. And come on, an edible plant with erect stems. How could I not? After examining the list of stimulants over and over, ginger, garlic, and coconut milk kept standing out (I've italicized other ingredients used in my menu), and incorporating asparagus into a curry only made sense.

The most labor-intensive aspect of this dish was making the curry from scratch. After that was done, I oven-roasted the asparagus to bring out its natural sweetness. Next, I slowly simmered paper-thin sweet potatoes in the curry until meltingly tender. Then I added the roasted asparagus and simmered briefly at the end. I envisioned a twist of fresh black pepper and a sprinkling of minced cilantro pulling everything together into a cohesive zip-pow-bang in my imaginary date's mouth.

It only made sense to round off the meal with turmeric-coated basmati for sopping up curry sauce and a sweet lassi to provide sweet, creamy interludes between spicy bites.

Masala Chai

I actually prefer this spiced Indian tea to coffee for a morning pick-me-up. Gets me going without making me jittery. This version takes around two hours to make, so I typically prepare it the night before I want to enjoy it. I suggest 1 teaspoon to 1 tablespoon of freshly grated ginger, so you should add an amount that suits your desire for spiciness. I typically use 2 teaspoons. If you have a mortar and pestle, combine the cardamom pods, cloves, and peppercorns and pound until fine, then transfer the mixture to the saucepan to simmer with water. I use black tea with dried orange peel to give this tea fresh citrus notes, but any black tea will do. Big thanks to Erin Cooney for chai-making tips.

YIELD
6 to 8 servings

SOUNDTRACK
"One Drop" by Bob Marley and the Wailers from *Survival*

BOOK
Water: The Epic Struggle for Wealth, Power, and Civilization by Steven Solomon

FILM
A Drop of Life directed by Shalini Kantayya

12 cups water

1 (2-inch) cinnamon stick

40 cardamom pods, cracked open

1 teaspoon whole cloves

1 teaspoon whole white and crushed black peppercorns

6 cups soy or almond milk

1 teaspoon to 1 tablespoon coarsely grated fresh ginger

2 bags or 2 heaping tablespoons loose black tea

6 tablespoons raw cane sugar, or to taste

In a medium-size saucepan over high heat, combine the water and the cinnamon stick and bring to a boil. Lower the heat to medium-high, add the cardamom, cloves, and pepper and simmer, strongly, until the amount of water is reduced by half, 45 minutes to 1 hour (I measure the height of the water with a wooden spoon and boil until the water has reduced by half that height).

Add the soy milk, raise the heat to high, and bring to a boil. Quickly lower the heat to medium-low and simmer, gently, until the amount of water is reduced by one-fourth, 45 minutes to 1 hour. Stir occasionally.

Add the ginger, raise the heat to medium-high, and simmer strongly, for 10 minutes.

Remove from the heat, add the tea and sugar, cover, and steep for at least 10 minutes. Strain the tea of solids, and serve hot.

Aromatic Asparagus and Sweet Potato Curry with Cilantro

Because asparagus spears, like most vegetables, start losing nutrients and flavor immediately after they are harvested, buy them at your nearest farmers' market when they make their grand appearance this year. Trust me, you don't want to miss out on one bit of the vitamin C, potassium, B vitamins, copper, vitamin A, iron, phosphorus, and zinc.

YIELD
4 to 6 servings

SOUNDTRACK
"Culture Move" by Asian Dub Foundation from *Rafi's Revenge*

BOOK
Orientalism by Edward Said

Coarse sea salt
2 bunches of asparagus, trimmed
2 tablespoons plus 2 teaspoons coconut oil
½ teaspoon yellow mustard seeds
1 medium-size yellow onion, diced finely
3 garlic cloves, minced
1 teaspoon minced fresh ginger
2 teaspoons Garam Masala (page 8)
½ teaspoon chili powder
1 teaspoon powdered turmeric
2 bay leaves
1 (14-ounce) can diced tomatoes
1 (14-ounce) can coconut milk
1 large or 2 small sweet potatoes, peeled and sliced thinly
Freshly ground black pepper
¼ cup minced fresh cilantro

Preheat the oven to 400°F.

In a large pot over high heat, bring 4 quarts of water to a boil. Add 1 tablespoon of salt, boil for 1 minute, add the asparagus, and immediately turn off the heat. Let sit for 1 minute, then drain.

Transfer the asparagus to a large plate and toss with 2 teaspoons of the coconut oil to coat lightly.

Transfer the asparagus to a large baking sheet and roast in the oven until it starts to crisp, 8 to 10 minutes.

Remove from the oven, cut diagonally into 1-inch pieces, and set aside.

In a large sauté pan over medium heat, warm the remaining coconut oil. Add the mustard seeds and cook until they pop, 2 to 3 minutes. Next, add the onion and sauté for 5 to 7 minutes, until soft and translucent. Then add the garlic, ginger, Garam Masala, chili powder, turmeric, bay leaves, and 1 teaspoon sea salt and sauté for an additional 2 minutes. Remove from the heat and set aside.

Place the tomatoes and their juices in a large bowl. With clean hands, squeeze the tomatoes through your fingers to break them into smaller pieces. Transfer the tomatoes to the sauté pan with the onions and spices. Add the coconut milk, then fill the coconut milk can one-quarter full with water and stir it well to incorporate any coconut milk that may have been left behind. Add this to the sauté pan and mix well. Add the sweet potato and simmer over low heat for about 20 minutes, until it is tender and the sauce has thickened. Add the asparagus pieces, cover, and simmer for 1 minute. Remove from the heat.

Add salt and pepper to taste.

Garnish with cilantro, and serve immediately.

Saag Tofu

The inspiration for this dish comes from saag paneer, an Indian dish comprising spinach (saag) and blocks of curdled cheese (paneer). The firm-tender tofu is a perfect stand-in for paneer.

YIELD
4 to 6 servings

SOUNDTRACK
"Born Free" by M.I.A. from *MAYA*

BOOK
War Talk by Arundhati Roy

  1 pound extra-firm tofu (1 large cake)
  1 teaspoon ground cumin
  ¾ teaspoon ground turmeric
  ¾ teaspoon mustard seeds
  ½ teaspoon fennel seeds
    Coarse sea salt
  5 tablespoons extra-virgin olive oil
  2 pounds fresh spinach, washed and trimmed
  1 small yellow onion (about 1 cup), chopped finely
  1 teaspoon minced fresh ginger
  2 small green chiles, seeded and minced
  ½ teaspoon ground coriander
  1 teaspoon freshly ground black pepper
  4 large garlic cloves, minced
  1½ cups unflavored rice milk

Preheat the oven to 450°F.

Place the tofu cake on its side and slice in half. Lay the tofu down flat, keeping the layers together, and slice it, widthwise, into three even slabs. Slice each of those slabs into quarters widthwise, leaving you with twenty-four cubes. Set aside.

In a large mixing bowl combine ½ teaspoon of cumin, ½ teaspoon of turmeric, ½ teaspoon of mustard seeds, ¼ teaspoon of fennel seeds, and ½ teaspoon of salt and mix well with a fork. Add

2 tablespoons of olive oil and mix well. Add the tofu cubes and *gently* toss to coat with the mixture.

Gently transfer the tofu cubes to a parchment-lined baking sheet in a single layer.

Roast for 30 minutes, *gently* turning with fork after 15 minutes.

While the tofu is roasting, combine 3 quarts of water and 1 teaspoon of salt in a large pot and bring to a boil. Add the spinach and blanch until softened, about 1 minute, drain in a colander, and chill under cold running water. Squeeze the water out of the spinach with a clean kitchen towel, then chop coarsely and set aside.

In a medium-size saucepan, combine the onion with the remaining olive oil and the ginger, chile, coriander, and black pepper, and the remaining ½ teaspoon of ground cumin, ¼ teaspoon of turmeric, ¼ teaspoon of mustard seeds, ¼ teaspoon of fennel seeds, and ¼ teaspoon of salt. Sauté over medium heat for 10 minutes, stirring often, until the vegetables are soft and browning. Add the garlic and cook for an additional 2 minutes.

Add the spinach and the rice milk to the saucepan and simmer over medium-low heat, covered, for about 15 minutes, until the spinach is creamy. Add eight to twelve tofu cubes to the spinach, avoiding overcrowding the spinach with tofu, and simmer for 5 more minutes (reserve the additional tofu for later use in another dish). Season with additional salt if necessary. Serve hot.

Yellow Basmati Rice

A simple way to brighten the color of plain basmati rice and add a faint pepper flavor is by cooking it in turmeric powder, a spice commonly used in South Asian and Middle Eastern cooking. The rice is perfect for soaking up the sauce of curries.

YIELD
4 to 6 servings

SOUNDTRACK
"Butterfly" by Talvin Singh from *O.K.*

BOOK
Stolen Harvest: The Hijacking of the Global Food Supply by Vandana Shiva

1 cup short-grain brown rice, soaked in water overnight

1 tablespoon extra-virgin olive oil

1 cup finely diced yellow onion
  Coarse sea salt

1 teaspoon turmeric

Drain the rice into a colander and set aside.

In a medium-size saucepan over low heat, combine the olive oil, onion, and ½ teaspoon of salt and sauté until well caramelized, 10 to 15 minutes. Add the turmeric and stir until well incorporated, about 30 seconds. Add the rice and cook for about 2 minutes, stirring often, until the water has evaporated and the rice starts to smell nutty.

Stir in 2¼ cups of water, bring to a boil, cover, lower the heat to low, and cook for 50 minutes.

Remove from the heat and steam with the lid on for at least 10 minutes, then fluff with a fork before serving.

YIELD
4 to 6 servings

SOUNDTRACK
"First Love" (Pratham Mix) by
Anoushka Shankar from *Anoushka*

BOOK
Siddhartha by Hermann Hesse

Cardamom-Saffron Sweet Lassi with Candied Cashews

This version of lassi—a traditional North Indian beverage made by blending yogurt with water, spices, and sometimes fruit—is mainly colored and flavored by saffron, a spice derived from the flower of the saffron crocus (Crocus sativus). Cardamom, the aromatic seeds of a plant of the ginger family, adds additional stimulation. I typically use coconut milk yogurt, but feel free to use whatever kind you prefer.

Candied Cashews

      2 cups raw cashews
      2 tablespoons light olive oil
    ¼ cup raw cane sugar

Lassi

      8 whole cardamom pods
    ¼ teaspoon saffron threads
    1½ cups boiling water
    3½ cups plain vegan yogurt
      6 tablespoons Simple Syrup (page 30), or 4 to 5
         tablespoons agave nectar
      3 tablespoons freshly squeezed lemon juice

For the candied cashews

In a large mixing bowl, combine the cashews with the olive oil and stir until thoroughly coated. Add the sugar and stir until thoroughly coated.

Warm a large, heavy cast-iron skillet to medium-high heat. Place the cashews in the skillet, scraping the bowl to remove everything, and stir constantly until the cashews are fragrant and most of the liquid has evaporated, about 1½ minutes.

Transfer cashews to parchment paper and quickly spread out, separating them with two forks. Set aside to cool. After they have cooled, roughly chop them.

For the lassi

Crack open the cardamom pods, emptying their seeds and the pods into a small bowl. Add the saffron threads and the boiling water. Stir well, and set aside until the liquid has cooled to room temperature, about 15 minutes.

With a fork, remove the cardamom pods from the water and discard, leaving the seeds in the water.

In an upright blender, combine the reserved cardamom water, yogurt, Simple Syrup, and lemon juice. Blend for 30 seconds to mix well. Garnish each serving with a heaping tablespoon of candied cashews, reserving the rest for another use.

crimson cookout

♀

cherry sangria

red beet tapenade crostini

strawberry gazpacho shooters with crispy rosemary

*open-faced grilled eggplant, red onion,
and heirloom tomato sandwiches with creamy celeriac sauce*

bright-black fingerling potatoes with fresh plum-tomato ketchup

raspberry-lime ice pops

SOUNDTRACK
Verve Remixed
Ella and Louis by Ella Fitzgerald and Louis Armstrong
The Astrud Gilberto Album by Astrud Gilberto
Swingin' Easy by Sarah Vaughan
Dinah Jams by Dinah Washington

Teaching kids how to feed themselves and how to live in a community responsibly is the center of an education.

—ALICE WATERS

The idea for this menu came from a dream I had about my daughter before she was born. In it she was an adult carrying on my vision of building community through food.

Picture this: apricot colored sun slowly fading away; garden torches flickering; moody downtempo wafting through the balmy air. Playing: the United Future Organization remix of Sarah Vaughan's "Summertime."

*Summertime
And the living is easy
Fish are jumpin'
And the cotton is high*

Stylish and affable guests chat as they nibble red beet tapenade crostini and help themselves to passed strawberry gazpacho soup shooters—quick-fried rosemary leaves floating at the top of each shot glass. A professor of Middle East and Islamic studies enlightens a third-year law student on the roots of the 2011 Egyptian revolution. Longtime friends from middle school clown each other over embarrassing blunders while adolescents. Tight eyed and giddy in a far corner of the backyard, a couple of old heads quietly take in everything.

The last few sips of cherry sangria are polished off, and pint-size canning jars are refilled. Anticipation builds as the final dishes are placed on the long, rustic wooden table. Mila, the brilliant and elegant host, removes her Cajun spice–coated potatoes from the oven inside the kitchen of her Mediterranean bungalow.

As she makes her way through the carefree crowd of friends with blackened fingerlings heaped in a red ceramic serving bowl, her father pulls the last slices of charred eggplant from the grill. Her radiant mother garnishes the creamy dressing with minced parsley and sets it on the table. All of the meal's elements coalesce to form a stunning crimson-hued buffet.

Flanked by her parents, Mila is visibly pleased, her smile widening as everyone circles around the table, holding hands.

edibleschoolyard.org • *whatsonyourplateproject.org*

Cherry Sangria

There is one key thing to remember when making sangria: What you put into it, you get out of it. So if you use red wine that you wouldn't thoroughly enjoy on its own, the quality of your sangria will suffer. I will admit that this is more expensive than your average sangria. But your friends will appreciate the investment. If you have them, use in-season cherries, but frozen cherries work just as well.

YIELD
Enough to keep you and your guests "nice" for the evening

SOUNDTRACK
"Summertime" by B. B. Seaton from *In Fine Style*

BOOKS
When Angels Speak of Love by bell hooks

Manifest Your Destiny: The Nine Spiritual Principles for Getting Everything You Want by Wayne Dyer

    3 (2-inch) cinnamon sticks
    1 cup freshly squeezed orange juice
    2 bottles good-quality red wine
    ¾ cup brandy
    ¼ cup Grand Marnier
    ¼ cup Cointreau
    ¼ cup agave nectar
       Lots of cherries, stemmed, pitted, and halved

Combine all the ingredients in a large nonreactive bowl or container, mix well, cover, and refrigerate for at least 6 hours or overnight.

YIELD
32 pieces

SOUNDTRACK
"Summertime" by Miles Davis from
Porgy and Bess

BOOKS
Salvation: Black People and Love by bell
hooks

You Can Heal Your Life by Louise Hay
with illustrations by Joan Perrin
Falquet

Red Beet Tapenade Crostini

I'm so happy my dear friend Laura Loescher suggested that I create a recipe for a beet-based tapenade. In addition to eating this sweet-tangy spread with rustic bread, it can be enjoyed with crackers and vegetables. I even use it as a condiment, slathering it on sandwiches. Any leftovers can be covered and refrigerated for 2 to 3 days.

2 garlic cloves, minced

2 tablespoons extra-virgin olive oil

1 cup packed roughly chopped Marinated Beets (page 29)

¼ cup packed pitted kalamata olives

1 tablespoon drained capers

1½ tablespoons freshly squeezed lemon juice

1 teaspoon minced fresh basil

Fine sea salt

Freshly ground white pepper

1 large baguette, sliced thinly

Combine the garlic and olive oil in a small sauté pan. Sauté over medium-low heat just until the garlic smells fragrant, about 2 minutes. Remove from the heat and set aside to cool.

Preheat the oven to 400°F.

In a food processor fitted with a metal blade, combine the beets, olives, capers, lemon juice, basil, and the cooled garlic oil. Pulse until smooth, scraping down the bowl to ensure all the beets are pureed. Season with salt and pepper to taste.

Place the baguette slices on a large baking sheet and bake until lightly browned and toasted, 6 to 10 minutes.

Spread the toasts with the tapenade and serve on a large platter.

Strawberry Gazpacho Shooters with Crispy Rosemary

Don't let the thought of strawberries in this soup throw you off. This rosemary-strawberry gazpacho is by no means a dessert. The earthy, fragrant rosemary oil helps this soup straddle the line between sweet and savory. Obviously, this soup can be served in a bowl for a light sit-down meal in the height of summer. But serving it in shot glasses is a great way for people to enjoy it at a larger party. It should go without saying that this soup is best when made with perfectly ripe, in-season strawberries.

YIELD
6 to 8 regular servings, or about 32 shooters

SOUNDTRACK
"Summertime" by Scarlett Johansson from *Unexpected Dreams—Songs from the Stars*

BOOKS
The Art of Seduction by Robert Greene
Think and Grow Rich by Napoleon Hill

Crispy Rosemary

- 3 tablespoons extra-virgin olive oil
- 4 (4-inch) rosemary sprigs, rosemary leaves removed from the stems

Strawberry Gazpacho

- ¼ cup raw organic cane sugar
  Coarse sea salt
- 3½ pounds strawberries, stemmed
- 1 medium-size red bell pepper, seeded and diced finely
- ¼ cup drained, finely diced Hot Pickled Red Onions (page 16)
- 1 cup freshly squeezed orange juice
- 2 tablespoons red wine vinegar
- 6 cups filtered water

For the crispy rosemary

In a medium-size saucepan over high heat, warm the olive oil until hot and just starting to smoke, 2 to 3 minutes. Quickly turn off the heat and add the rosemary to the hot oil. Cook until crispy, shaking the pan to ensure that all the rosemary is covered in hot oil, about 3 minutes. Strain the oil into a large mixing bowl. Set the crispy rosemary aside.

For the strawberry gazpacho

Immediately add the sugar and 1 teaspoon of salt to the bowl with the rosemary oil and mix well until dissolved. Set aside.

Remove 2 cups of strawberries from the 3½ pounds and set the remaining strawberries aside. Finely dice the 2 cups. Transfer to the bowl with the rosemary oil mixture, and add the bell pepper, onions, orange juice, and red wine vinegar. Gently mix well and set aside.

Puree the remaining strawberries and the water in an upright blender (in batches if necessary) or with an immersion blender. Strain through a medium mesh strainer into the bowl with the diced strawberry mixture. Discard the strawberry seeds. Stir well to incorporate the puree.

Refrigerate for at least 2 hours.

Season with more salt to taste, if necessary.

To serve, ladle the soup into chilled shot glasses or bowls, and garnish with several crispy rosemary leaves.

Open-Faced Grilled Eggplant, Red Onion, and Heirloom Tomato Sandwiches with Creamy Celeriac Sauce

While a slice of rustic bread supports the vegetables on this open-faced sandwich, grilled eggplant is the real foundation. Grilled eggplant has a sweet, smoky flavor and would be delicious eaten alone. But I layer tangy-sweet grilled onions and ripe, seasonal heirloom tomatoes into the mix to add beautiful colors and additional flavors that meld well with the buttery eggplant. Right before serving, the sandwich is brightened with Creamy Celeriac Sauce.

If you can't grill, the eggplant and onions can also be cooked in an oven. Just place them on a parchment-lined baking sheet 3 to 4 inches from the heat and broil for 3 to 4 minutes, until browned and slightly crisp. Turn them with a fork and broil for another minute or so. After removing the vegetables, place the bread under the broiler for about 1½ minutes per side, until lightly browned.

Creamy Celeriac Sauce

- ½ pound silken tofu
- 2 tablespoons freshly squeezed lemon juice
- 2 tablespoons minced fresh parsley
- 1 garlic clove, minced
- ½ teaspoon agave nectar
- ½ teaspoon Dijon mustard
- 2 tablespoons extra-virgin olive oil
- ½ teaspoon paprika
  A few pinches of cayenne
  Coarse sea salt
  Freshly ground white pepper
- ¼ cup minced green onions (green and white parts)
- ½ cup loosely packed peeled and coarsely grated celery root (celeriac)

YIELD
8 servings

SOUNDTRACK
"Summertime" by John Coltrane from *My Favorite Things*

BOOKS
Mindful Loving by Henry Grayson

The Seven Spiritual Laws of Success: A Practical Guide to the Fulfillment of Your Dreams by Deepak Chopra

Sandwiches

¼ cup extra-virgin olive oil
1 teaspoon coarse sea salt
¼ teaspoon cayenne
½ teaspoon freshly ground black pepper
1 medium-size eggplant (about 1 pound), sliced crosswise into ½-inch rounds
2 medium-size red onions, sliced crosswise into ½-inch rounds
4 heirloom tomatoes, cut crosswise into ½-inch slices
1 loaf of rustic bread cut diagonally into eight ½-inch slices
Freshly ground white pepper
Fine sea salt

For the sauce

In an upright blender, combine the tofu, lemon juice, 1 tablespoon of the parsley, garlic, agave nectar, mustard, olive oil, paprika, cayenne, ½ teaspoon of salt, and ¼ teaspoon of pepper and blend until smooth. If necessary, season with additional salt and pepper to taste.

Transfer the sauce to a bowl, stir in the green onions and celery root, and garnish with the remaining parsley.

For the sandwiches

Preheat a grill or broiler. Soak eight 12-inch wooden skewers in water for at least 30 minutes.

In a mixing bowl, combine the olive oil, salt, cayenne, and black pepper and mix well with a fork.

Add the vegetables to the bowl and toss to coat.

If grilling, thread the onion slices onto two skewers each. Transfer the onions and the eggplant rounds to the grill and cook, turning once with tongs, until browned and slightly crisp, 3 to 4 minutes per side.

After turning the vegetables, add the bread to the grill. Cook, turning once, until crisp and golden on the surface but still soft inside, about 4 minutes.

Assemble the sandwich by layering a slice of eggplant, a slice of tomato, and several slices of onion. Slather on some celeriac sauce, then sprinkle with salt and pepper before serving.

YIELD
8 to 10 servings

SOUNDTRACK
"Summertime" by Angélique Kidjo
from *The Best of Angélique Kidjo*

BOOKS
Getting the Love You Want: A Guide for Couples by Harville Hendrix

The Dynamic Laws of Prosperity by Catherine Ponder

Bright-Black Fingerling Potatoes with Fresh Plum-Tomato Ketchup

Blackening is a Cajun cooking technique that involves coating food with a mixture of dried herbs and spices. The herb and spice blend in this recipe turns run-of-the-mill potatoes into flavor bombs. I enjoy them with Plum-Tomato Ketchup, and they taste good with the Creamy Celeriac Sauce (page 81), too. If you can't find fingerlings, you can use small new potatoes that have been sliced in half lengthwise, then cut into three even, lengthwise slices.

4 pounds fingerling potatoes, washed, scrubbed, dried with a clean towel, and halved lengthwise

3 tablespoons extra-virgin olive oil

1 tablespoon paprika

1 teaspoon onion powder

1 teaspoon garlic powder

1 teaspoon chili powder

1 teaspoon ground cumin

1 teaspoon ground coriander

Pinch of cayenne, or more to taste

3 tablespoons minced fresh thyme

1½ teaspoon fine sea salt

1 teaspoon freshly ground white pepper

Plum-Tomato Ketchup (page 26)

Preheat oven to 450°F.

In a large bowl, combine the potatoes and 1 tablespoon of the oil. Toss well to coat.

Arrange the potatoes, cut side down, on two parchment-lined baking sheets, and roast for 20 minutes, stirring after 10 minutes.

While the potatoes are roasting, combine the spices and herbs in a small bowl and mix well with a fork. Set aside.

Transfer the potatoes to a large mixing bowl, add the remaining oil, and toss well with a large spoon to coat. Add the spice blend to the bowl, toss well to coat, then transfer back to the baking sheet, cut side up.

Roast until the potatoes are tender and crisping, about 15 more minutes.

YIELD
6 to 8 ice pops

SOUNDTRACK
"Summertime" by DJ Jazzy Jeff and the Fresh Prince from *Homebase*

BOOK
Oh, the Places You'll Go! by Dr. Seuss

Raspberry-Lime Ice Pops

The raspberry and lime flavors are equally distinct in these bright, refreshing ice pops. I make them using store-bought molds, but using small cups works just as well. Simply add the prepared juice to the cup, cover it with paper, wrap a rubber band around the paper to hold it in place, poke an ice-pop stick in the center of the paper almost to the bottom of the cup, then freeze as directed. I have found that freezing beverages typically decreases their sweetness. So the juice for making these pops may seem sweet, but after they are frozen the taste will even out.

2 cups fresh raspberries
1½ cups filtered water
2 tablespoons freshly squeezed lime juice
½ cup raw cane sugar, or 6 tablespoons agave nectar
½ teaspoon lemon zest

In a small saucepan over medium heat, combine the raspberries, water, lime juice, sugar, and lemon zest. Simmer, stirring often, until the sugar is dissolved, the raspberries have softened, and the liquid is thick, about 10 minutes. Let cool for 5 minutes, then puree in two batches in a blender. Strain through a fine sieve or cheesecloth into a bowl, and refrigerate, covered, until completely chilled.

Pour the juice into 6 ice-pop molds (or cups with ice-pop sticks), leaving a ¼-inch space at the top to allow for expansion after freezing. After filling the molds, if there is any juice left over, water it down and enjoy. Place the pops in a freezer for at least 6 hours, until frozen completely.

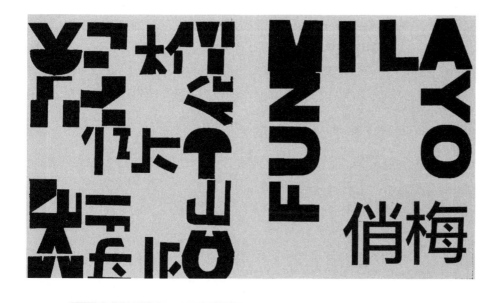

funmilayo's feast

bissap cooler

sliced cucumber and mint salad

funmilayo fritters with harissa

wet jollof rice with carrots, cabbage, and parsley-garlic paste

white wine–simmered collards with oven-dried tomatoes

thiakry with millet and raisins

SOUNDTRACK

Beautiful Imperfection by Asa

Black Voices by Tony Allen

Club Sodade by Cesária Évora

Troubadour by K'naan

From Africa with Fury: Rise by Seun Kuti

You should be ready at all times to seek the interest of the
poor and needy, always to speak the truth, no matter if it
will cost you all you have, and even your life.

—FUNMILAYO RANSOME-KUTI

In college I discovered the music of Fela Kuti, and I was immediately trans-
fixed by his rhythmic blend of funk, jazz, and African highlife—also known
as Afrobeat (thanks, Mr. Powell). I remember bumping "Colonial Mentality"
for the first time as I drove to the French Quarter, hyperactively bouncing in
my seat the whole way. In fact, the first half-dozen times I played Fela's songs
I could not stop moving. My response was almost Pavlovian. When I finally
slowed down enough to give Fela's music a close listening, I discovered that
it was layered with pointed political messages.

Fela's political views and music took a radical turn after he visited the
United States in 1969 and learned about the Black Power movement. When
he and his band returned to Nigeria they created some of the most compelling protest songs to come out of Africa, addressing everything from gov-
ernment corruption within Africa to the exploitation of natural resources on
the continent by multinational corporations. Listening to Fela's music had a
tremendous impact on my thoughts around African history, capitalism, im-
perialism, and the power of music to enlighten.

Several years later, my friend Dani mentioned that Fela Kuti was a son of
one of Nigeria's most respected political activists—Funmilayo Ransome-
Kuti. Up until that point, all the contemporary revolutionaries from Africa
that I had heard of were men, such as Kwame Nkrumah, Sékou Touré, Patrice
Lumumba, Amílcar Cabral, and other leaders of African liberation movements. So I was excited to find out about "The Mother of Africa," as Funmilayo
Ransome-Kuti is often called. I learned that she was a teacher, anticolonial activist, and politician who worked tirelessly for the equal rights of Nigerian
women as well as the human rights of all Nigerians until she died in 1978. It
only made sense that Fela (as well as his two brothers) was an outspoken
human rights activist.

After seeing the Broadway production of *Fela!* in 2010 and telling my wife how excited I was that the story prominently featured Fela's mother and her influence on him, we ordered *For Women and the Nation*, the only full-length biography of Funmilayo Ransome-Kuti. My wife was so inspired by Funmilayo Ransome-Kuti's life and legacy, when it was time to choose a name for our daughter, she suggested Funmilayo. I immediately agreed.

The usual full version of this Yoruba name is Oluwafunmilayo, which means "God has given me joy." It will bring us joy if our daughter is inspired by her namesake's courage, radicalism, and commitment to justice. This menu, influenced by the cuisine of Algeria, Nigeria, and Senegal, is dedicated to Funmilayo Ransome-Kuti, my daughter—Funmilayo Chiu Mui Terry-Koon—and all the nameless and faceless mothers and daughters throughout the African diaspora who have worked to create a better world.

greenbeltmovement.org • *viacampesina.org*

YIELD
About ½ gallon

SOUNDTRACK
"New Africa" by Youssou N'Dour from
I Bring What I Love

BOOK
The Collected Poetry by Léopold Sédar
Senghor

Bissap Cooler

Bissap, the national drink of Senegal, is simply a tea of dried hibiscus flowers (Hibiscus sabdariffa*) that has (typically) been sweetened. This version starts with a hibiscus concentrate that is brightened with sparkling water to give the drink a refreshing fizz. Fun fact: Hibiscus tea is known to reduce high blood pressure.*

    4 cups water
    1 cup (about 1 ounce) dried hibiscus
    ½ cup coarsely grated fresh ginger
    ¾ cup raw cane sugar, or ½ cup agave, or more to taste
    5 tablespoons freshly squeezed lime juice
    5 cups almost frozen sparkling water, or more to taste
    ½ large organic lime, ends cut off and sliced thinly
       lengthwise, for garnish

In a large saucepan over high heat, combine the 4 cups of water with the hibiscus, ginger, and sugar. Bring to a boil, lower the heat to medium, and simmer, covered, for 10 minutes, stirring a few times. Remove from the heat and steep for 10 minutes. Uncover, stir in the lime juice, and set aside to cool.

Strain the drink into a pitcher, pressing down on the solids to extract all their liquids, and refrigerate until cold. Discard the solids.

Immediately before serving, add the sparkling water and *gently* stir to combine.

Serve in tall slender glasses garnished with lime slices. Guests should feel free to add more sparkling water to taste.

Sliced Cucumber and Mint Salad

While doing research for this book, I ran across Salade de Concombre à la Menthe, an Algerian dish that Jessica B. Harris shares in The Africa Cookbook. *Her recipe reminded me of the Cucumber, Mint, and Lime Salad from my first book,* Grub. *The salad in this menu is a hybrid of these two.*

Cucumber salads are refreshing and cooling on hot summer days, and this one can be enjoyed by itself as an afternoon snack, added to a summer salad buffet, or eaten as a prelude to Funmilayo's Feast. If eaten as a part of this menu, I would serve it to guests as a welcoming appetizer as the fritters are being cooked.

YIELD
4 to 6 servings

SOUNDTRACK
"Alkher Illa Doffor / Ad Izayanugass" by Cheb I Sabbah from *La Kehena*

FILM
The Battle of Algiers directed by Gillo Pontecorvo

2 large seedless cucumbers, peeled and sliced thinly
2 tablespoons freshly squeezed lemon juice
3 tablespoons minced fresh mint
 Coarse sea salt

In a medium-size bowl, combine the cucumbers, lemon juice, and mint. With clean hands, toss for about 1 minute. Add ¼ teaspoon of salt. Cover and refrigerate for at least 30 minutes, or up to 2 hours. Bring to room temperature before serving, and add more salt, if necessary.

YIELD
24 to 26 fritters

SOUNDTRACK
"Fleurette Africaine" by Duke Ellington
with Charles Mingus and Max Roach
from *Money Jungle*

BOOKS
*For Women and the Nation: Funmilayo
Ransome-Kuti of Nigeria* by Cheryl
Johnson-Odim and Nina Emma

Famished Road by Ben Okri

Funmilayo Fritters with Harissa

Bean fritters deep-fried in oil may have originated in West Africa, but they pop up throughout the African diaspora. These crunchy white bean fritters, known as akara, are a distinctive dish of Nigeria. So it only makes sense to dedicate them to Funmilayo Ransome-Kuti. Although these beans should be soaked overnight (as you would in other dishes that use dried beans), they do not need to be precooked. After being fried until golden brown they are ready to go. Well, almost ready. They wouldn't be complete without my version of harissa, a chili sauce commonly eaten in North Africa. Now they're ready. In many cases these would be eaten as an appetizer, but I imagine them being central to this menu, eaten in a bowl with the jolof rice and greens. By the way, the peanuts can be omitted from the fritters for those with peanut allergies.

1	cup dried great northern beans, soaked overnight, drained, and rinsed
½	medium-size onion, chopped finely
1	cup roasted peanuts without skin
¼	teaspoon cayenne
1	tablespoon apple cider vinegar
¼	cup plus 2 tablespoons filtered water
1	teaspoon fine sea salt
1	tablespoon cornmeal
1	tablespoon minced fresh thyme
	Enough coconut oil for deep-frying (about 2 cups in a small saucepan)
	Harissa (page 9)

In a food processor fitted with a metal blade, combine the beans, onion, peanuts, cayenne, vinegar, water, and salt and pulse until completely smooth. Transfer to a medium-size bowl, cover, and refrigerate for 1 hour.

Preheat the oven to 200°F.

Remove the batter from the refrigerator, add the cornmeal and thyme, and beat with a wooden spoon for 2 minutes.

In a small saucepan over high heat, warm the oil until hot but not smoking, about 5 minutes.

Lower the heat to medium-high. Scoop a heaping tablespoon of batter, roll it in your hand into the shape of a walnut, transfer to a spoon, and gently drop into the oil. Fry in batches of four, stirring around after 2 minutes, until golden brown, 4 to 5 minutes. If necessary, adjust the temperature to ensure that the fritters do not cook too quickly.

I find that four to five fritters per person is usually sufficient. You can always freeze any leftover batter for later use.

Transfer the fritters to a paper towel–lined plate and allow them to drain. Next, transfer them to a baking sheet, and place in the oven to keep warm.

Serve with the Harissa.

YIELD
4 to 6 servings

SOUNDTRACK
"A Song for Women" by Baaba Maal
from *Television*

BOOK
*Les Bouts de Bois de Dieu (God's Bits of
Wood)* by Sembene Ousmane

Wet Jollof Rice with Carrots, Cabbage, and Parsley-Garlic Paste

Thiéboudienne—the national dish of Senegal, West Africa—is marinated fish cooked with tomato paste and a variety of vegetables served with Jollof rice, a dish composed of long-grain rice, tomatoes, onions, and spices. The fish is usually stuffed with parsley-garlic paste (called roff) to add flavor. In my version of Jollof rice I use short-grain brown rice to give the dish an almost sticky texture. The "wetness" comes from added tomato sauce, which makes it lean toward a thick stew. This consistency makes it perfect for eating with Funmilayo Fritters (with your hands, take a piece of the fritter and scoop up some rice). Before serving, I add a few dollops of parsley-garlic paste to round off the flavors in this dish.

Parsley-Garlic Paste

1 large bunch of parsley, trimmed
3 large garlic cloves, minced
½ teaspoon coarse sea salt
1 tablespoon extra-virgin olive oil

Rice

1 cup short-grain brown rice, soaked in water overnight
3 tablespoons peanut or extra-virgin olive oil
1 cup finely diced yellow onion
1 teaspoon chili powder
¼ teaspoon cayenne
1 large jalapeño, seeded and cut into ¼-inch dice
4 garlic cloves, minced
2 cups chopped canned tomato with their juices
1 tablespoon tomato paste
Coarse sea salt
2 cups Vegetable Stock (page 4)
2 cups ½-inch-diced carrots
4 medium-size wedges savoy cabbage
3 tablespoons fresh minced thyme

For the parsley-garlic paste

In a food processor fitted with a metal blade, combine the parsley, garlic, salt, and oil and pulse (pushing down the mixture with a rubber spatula) until well combined. You can also pound it into a paste with a mortar and pestle. Set aside.

For the rice

Drain the rice and set aside.

In a medium-size saucepan over low heat, combine the peanut oil, onion, chili powder, and cayenne and sauté until well caramelized, 10 to 15 minutes. Add the jalapeño and garlic and cook until fragrant, about 1½ minutes. Add the rice and cook for about 2 minutes, stirring often, until the water has evaporated and the rice starts to smell nutty.

Stir in the tomatoes and their juices, the tomato paste, ½ teaspoon of salt, and the vegetable stock. Bring to a boil, stir in the carrots to incorporate, and gently push the four cabbage wedges to the bottom of the rice, keeping them intact (it is okay if some cabbage is sticking out). Cover, lower the heat to low, and cook for 50 minutes.

Remove from the heat, sprinkle the thyme over the rice, and steam, covered, for at least 10 minutes.

YIELD
4 to 6 servings

SOUNDTRACK
"Colonial Mentality" by Fela Kuti from
Zombie

BOOKS
How Europe Underdeveloped Africa by
Walter Rodney

Things Fall Apart by Chinua Achebe

White Wine–Simmered Collard Greens with Oven-Dried Tomatoes

This can be eaten as a side dish. But I added it to this menu to be eaten in a bowl with the Jollof rice. The tanginess of the Oven-Dried Tomatoes balances the slightly bitter collards.

Coarse sea salt

2 large bunches collard greens, ribs removed and cut into bite-size pieces

2 teaspoons extra-virgin olive oil

2 large garlic cloves, minced

1 cup oven-dried (page 24) or sun-dried tomatoes (unsalted), drained (if in oil), sliced thinly, and squeezed with a clean kitchen towel

¼ cup white wine

In a large pot over high heat, bring 3 quarts of water to a boil and add 1 tablespoon of salt. Add the collards and cook, uncovered, for 4 to 6 minutes, until softened.

Prepare a large bowl of ice water to shock the collards.

Remove the collards from the heat, drain, and plunge them into the bowl of cold water to stop cooking and set their color. Drain.

In a medium-size sauté pan over medium heat, warm the oil. Add the garlic and sauté for 1 minute. Add the collards, Oven-Dried Tomatoes, and ¼ teaspoon of salt. Sauté for 3 minutes, stirring frequently.

Add the white wine, stir to incorporate, cover, and sauté for 15 seconds. Turn off the heat and steam for a few minutes. Season with additional salt to taste, if necessary.

Thiakry with Millet and Raisins

I first learned about Thiakry at Joloff, a Senegalese restaurant in my old Brooklyn neighborhood. The modern version of this West African dessert often combines couscous with yogurt and sugar. More traditional versions of this dish use the whole-grain millet, which I use here. Thompson raisins and agave nectar provide sweetness. Although I prefer using coconut yogurt as the base of my version, you should feel free to use whatever vegan yogurt you enjoy most. I prefer to drink this dessert as one would kefir, a thick drink made from fermented milk.

YIELD
4 to 6 servings

SOUNDTRACK
"Petite Fleur" by Angélique Kidjo from *Oyo*

BOOK
Mama Miti: Wangari Maathai and the Trees of Kenya by Donna Jo Napoli with illustrations by Kadir Nelson

Pinch of fine sea salt

3 tablespoons millet

¼ cup Thompson raisins

2 cups plain vegan yogurt

½ cup unflavored rice milk

1 tablespoon freshly squeezed lemon juice

½ teaspoon vanilla extract

1 tablespoon agave nectar (or preferred sweetener), or more to taste

In a medium-size saucepan over high heat, bring ½ cup of water to a boil. Immediately stir in the salt and millet, lower the heat to low, cover, and simmer for 20 minutes. Remove from the heat and let steam, covered for 10 minutes. Remove the lid, and cool.

In the meantime, place the raisins in a heatproof bowl. Add enough boiling water to cover by an inch and set aside until soft and plump, about 5 minutes. Drain and discard the liquid. Set the raisins aside.

Next, combine the yogurt, rice milk, lemon juice, vanilla extract, agave, and reserved raisins in a medium-size bowl. Cover and refrigerate.

When the millet has cooled, fold into the yogurt mixture. Serve chilled and enjoy as you would a pudding.

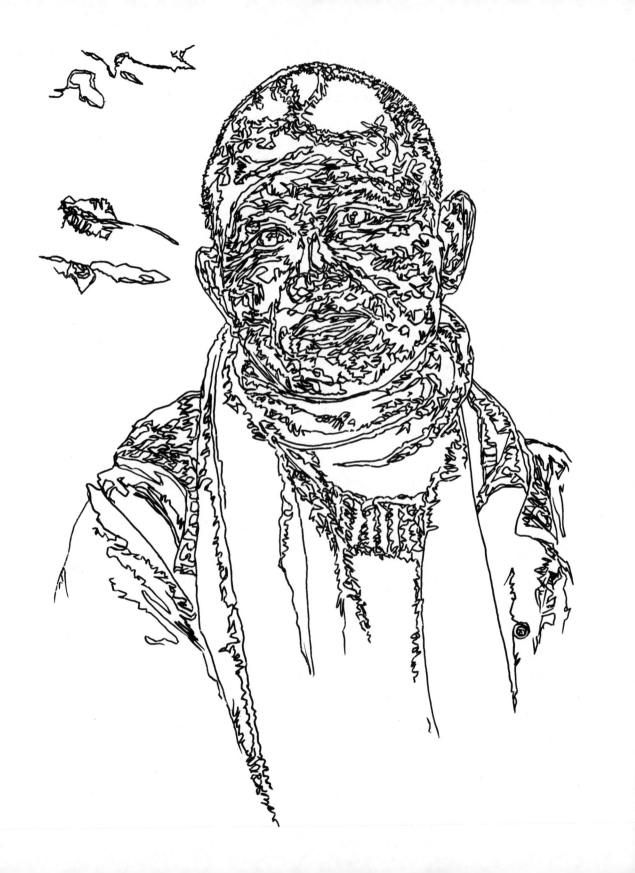

mindful brunch

ç

bloody sunday

ambrosia punch

crunchy chopped salad with creamy herb dressing

sweet potato–cornmeal drop biscuits with maple syrup

*velvety grits with sautéed summer squash,
heirloom tomatoes, and parsley-walnut pesto*

frozen café no lait with nutmeg and chocolate shavings

SOUNDTRACK

A Tribute to the King by Reverend James Cleveland

Precious Lord Recording of the Great Gospel Songs of Thomas A. Dorsey

Black, Brown, & Beige by Duke Ellington, featuring Mahalia Jackson

The Gold and Blue Album by the Fisk Jubilee Singers

Gospels, Spirituals, and Hymns by Mahalia Jackson

I love to sit and eat quietly and enjoy each bite, aware of
the presence of my community, aware of all the hard and
loving work that has gone into my food. When I eat in
this way, not only am I physically nourished, I am also
spiritually nourished.

—THÍCH NHẤT HANH

Sundays are sacred to me. Yes, hallowed in the sense that I sometimes go to
church in the morning or sit with my meditation sangha in the evening. But
the day is sacrosanct for additional reasons: No matter how much is going on
in my life, during the twenty-four hours before Monday I am intentional about
putting away work, slowing down, and connecting. On Sundays, I also com-
municate with the divine by inhaling deeply, being silent for hours, fasting

from eating during the day, staring at the sky, hiking in the redwoods, and sharing meals with loved ones.

Growing up, especially in high school, Sundays were more complicated. I was pretty contemptuous of the mornings. They started at around eight thirty with my mom coming into my bedroom every ten minutes, saying the last two words that a teenage boy who spent the prior evening watching "movies" on Cinemax until 3 AM wanted to hear—"Get up!" After half an hour, my dad would pull the covers off my bed and tell me that he would deduct from my allowance if I didn't get ready for Mass *that* second. I took a rushed shower, ate the cold remnants of instant grits or soggy pancakes they left me, hurriedly put on a tie I didn't want to wear, and sulked the whole way to church.

I wouldn't say I despised Mass, but apart from the sweet swill that was served during communion, the only thing I looked forward to was its end. What I really anticipated, however, came shortly afterward. My parents would usually take us to Piccadilly (or Piccadilly's, as folks in Memphis call it), a chain of cafeteria restaurants that serve home-style Southern meals. Honestly, besides those bangin' sweet rolls, I don't recall anything in particular that I ever ate at Piccadilly. But those afternoons are some of the most joyous memories of my childhood.

Unlike the rushed, transactional dinners on school nights that were sandwiched between sports practice and homework, we took our time at lunch on Sunday. We lingered. We laughed. We learned about one another. After lunch, no matter how much I protested (I wanted go home and play Nintendo), my dad would insist that we go for a walk at our neighborhood park to "digest our food."

I like to think that those few hours after Mass were an extension of church for my family. After we spent the morning praying with heads bowed and palms pressed together, we observed communion in a different way—bridging the gap between eating and intimacy and satisfying two of our most primal needs at once. The way I see it, mindfully sharing a meal with loved ones on Sunday or any other day provides a beautiful opportunity to renew our interconnection with all living beings in one fell swoop. A prayer, indeed.

Bloody Sunday

This drink, inspired by the Bloody Mary, uses marinated beet puree as its base. I created it in honor of the six hundred freedom fighters that were marching on March 7, 1965, from Selma to Montgomery, Alabama, when they were attacked with billy clubs and tear gas by state and local lawmen. Seventeen marchers were hospitalized, leading to the naming of the day "Bloody Sunday."

- 4 tablespoons fresh beet juice or marinated beet puree (recipe follows)
- 3 tablespoons vodka
- 1 tablespoon freshly squeezed lemon juice
- ¼ teaspoon apple cider vinegar
  at least ¼ teaspoon of Crystal or Louisiana Hot Sauce (but more if you'd like)
  Pinch of fine sea salt
  Pinch of freshly ground white pepper
- 1 skewer of 2 wedges Marinated Beets (page 29)

Fill a cocktail shaker with ice and add the beet puree, vodka, lemon juice, vinegar, hot sauce, salt, and pepper. Vigorously shake the ingredients until well chilled.

Strain into a ½-pint canning jar filled with ice.

Garnish with the skewer of beet wedges.

Marinated Beet Puree

- 1 cup Marinated Beets (page 29)
- 1½ cups water

In an upright blender, combine the Marinated Beets with the water and blend until smooth.

Press the puree through a fine-mesh strainer into a jar that can be sealed.

YIELD
1 cocktail

SOUNDTRACK
"Sunday Bloody Sunday" by Saul Williams from *The Inevitable Rise and Liberation of NiggyTardust!*

BOOKS
The Wages of Whiteness: Race and the Making of the American Working Class

Working toward Whiteness: How America's Immigrants Became White: The Strange Journey from Ellis Island to the Suburbs both by David Roediger

FILM
Four Little Girls directed by Spike Lee

YIELD
About 1 cup (enough for 3 cocktails)

YIELD
6 to 12 servings

SOUNDTRACK
"In Bright Mansions" by the Fisk
Jubilee Singers from *In Bright
Mansions*

BOOK
*Righteous Discontent: The Women's
Movement in the Black Baptist
Church, 1880–1920* by Evelyn
Brooks Higginbotham

Ambrosia Punch

*One Christmas I offered to make a nonalcoholic drink for our family
dinner. Inspired by ambrosia, a fruit salad made of pineapple, mandarin oranges, and coconut, I came up with this drink.*

½ cup coconut milk

3 cups filtered water

2 cups freshly squeezed orange juice

6 tablespoons freshly squeezed lemon juice

1 teaspoon orange extract

½ cup Simple Syrup (page 30), or 6 tablespoons agave
nectar

2 oranges, sliced thinly

1 lemon, sliced thinly

In an upright blender, combine the coconut milk with ½ cup of
the water and blend well. Transfer to a large pitcher. Add the remaining water, orange juice, lemon juice, orange extract, and
Simple Syrup. Stir well to combine.

Cover and refrigerate.

Immediately before serving, stir well and add the sliced fruit.

Crunchy Chopped Salad with Creamy Herb Dressing

While I usually prefer colorful salads, I appreciate the beauty of this monotone mix of nutrient-dense vegetables and Fuji apple slices. Once you add the herb-rich dressing it is brimming with flavor, and the varied textures provide fulfilling crunchiness with every bite.

Dressing

- 2 tablespoons freshly squeezed lemon juice
- 2 tablespoons red wine vinegar
- 1 teaspoon Dijon mustard
- 1 large garlic clove, minced
- 1 tablespoon minced fresh herbs, such as tarragon, basil, parsley, or thyme
  Coarse sea salt
- ¼ cup soft silken tofu
- 2 tablespoons extra-virgin olive oil
  Freshly ground white pepper

Salad

- Coarse sea salt
- ¼ pound fresh green beans, snapped at each end and cut in ½-inch pieces
- 1 heart of romaine (about ½ pound), chopped into bite-size pieces
- 2 medium-size seedless cucumbers, peeled and cut into ½-inch dice
- 1 green bell pepper, seeded and cut into ¼-inch dice
- 1 celery rib, diced finely
- 2 green onions, minced
- 2 large Fuji apples, cored and sliced thinly

YIELD
4 to 6 servings

SOUNDTRACK
"Joshua Fit the Battle of Jericho" by Paul Robeson from *The Originals: Spirituals*

BOOK
Savor: Mindful Eating, Mindful Life by Thích Nhất Hạnh and Lilian Cheung

For the dressing

In an upright blender, combine the lemon juice, vinegar, mustard, garlic, herbs, ½ teaspoon of sea salt, and tofu. Blend while slowly adding the oil. Season with salt and pepper to taste. Set aside.

For the salad

Bring 3 quarts of water to a boil in a large pot over high heat and add 1 tablespoon of salt. Add the green beans and cook just until tender but still al dente, about 3 minutes. Drain the beans into a colander, and shock in a bowl filled with ice water to stop cooking. Drain again, pat with a clean kitchen towel, and place in a large serving bowl.

Add the remaining ingredients and mix well. Immediately before serving, add enough dressing to lightly coat the salad. Toss well to coat evenly.

Sweet Potato–Cornmeal Drop Biscuits with Maple Syrup

Peter Berley's Sweet Potato–Pecan Drop Biscuits inspired these biscuits. Because this cookbook would not be complete without at least one riff on a recipe from The Modern Vegetarian Kitchen. *The key is making a puree of sweet potato that gives the biscuits earthy sweetness. Although this is a breakfast menu, these biscuits go well at lunch and dinner, too.*

YIELD
Approximately 24 biscuits

SOUNDTRACK
"Steal Away" by Mahalia Jackson from
The Forgotten Recordings

BOOK
*Going Home: Jesus and Buddha as
Brothers* by Thích Nhất Hạnh

¾	cup whole wheat pastry flour
¾	cup unbleached all-purpose flour
½	cup cornmeal
2	teaspoons baking powder
½	teaspoon baking soda
¾	teaspoon fine sea salt
2	tablespoons raw organic sugar
5	tablespoons chilled coconut butter (solidified coconut oil)
½	cup sweet potato puree (recipe follows)
½	cup unflavored rice milk
1	tablespoon pure maple syrup
1	tablespoon apple cider vinegar

Preheat the oven to 425°F.

In a large bowl, sift together the flours, cornmeal, baking powder, baking soda, and salt. Stir in the sugar, and then rub the coconut butter into the flour mixture with your fingertips until the mixture resembles sand with pebbles.

In an upright blender, combine the sweet potato puree, rice milk, maple syrup, and apple cider vinegar and blend well. Then, make a well in the center of the flour pebbles, add the rice milk mixture, and stir just until the dough comes away from the sides of the bowl and the mixture is well blended, about 1 minute.

Drop walnut-size balls of dough from a spoon, giving the dough as much height as possible, onto a parchment-lined baking sheet and bake for 10 to 12 minutes, or until lightly browned.

YIELD
About ½ cup

Sweet Potato Puree

    1   cup peeled and diced sweet potatoes
    2   tablespoons water
        Coarse sea salt

Combine the sweet potatoes, 1 quart of cold water, and ¼ teaspoon of salt in a medium-size pot over high heat. Boil, uncovered, for 15 to 20 minutes, or until the sweet potatoes are easily pierced with a knife.

In a food processor fitted with a metal blade, combine the sweet potatoes with the 2 tablespoons of water and blend until smooth.

With rosemary-infused simple syrup and freshly squeezed grapefruit juice, this light and refreshing drink has a perfumy essence (page 42). Paprika gives these peanuts a tempting reddish-orange tint and a mildly smoky-sweet flavor (page 43).

Warm, creamy, and scrumptious, Savory Grits with Sautéed Broad Beans, Roasted Fennel, and Thyme will become a standard comfort food in your family's home. Broad beans give the dish an earthy richness, and the soft, melting texture of roasted fennel adds subtle complexity (page 44).

Ginger-Molasses Cake with Molasses-Coated Walnuts is rich, full of flavor, and unbelievably moist (page 48).

For Cherry Sangria use in-season cherries if you have them. But frozen cherries work just as well (page 77). Enjoy with sweet-tangy Red Beet Tapenade Crostini (page 78).

While slightly sweet, rosemary-strawberry gazpacho is by no means a dessert. Earthy, fragrant rosemary oil helps this soup straddle the line between sweet and savory (page 79).

These Open-Faced Grilled Eggplant, Red Onion, and Heirloom Tomato Sandwiches are brightened with Creamy Celeriac Sauce (page 35). I eat Bright-Black Fingerling Potatoes with Fresh Plum-Tomato Ketchup (page 84).

Raspberry and lime flavors are equally distinct in these bright, refreshing Raspberry-Lime Ice Pops (page 86).

The combination of simmered black-eyed peas and sautéed mustards in Black-Eyed Peas in Garlic-Ginger-Braised Mustard Greens is simple yet flavorful. There is just enough ginger to provide some warmth and subtle zing without overpowering this dish (page 143).

In Ida B. Limeade the sour juice of freshly squeezed limes is combined with cayenne and raw cane sugar. It is finished off with a tablespoon of beet puree to give this drink a beautiful light fuchsia hue (page 142).

This everyday version of candied sweet
potatoes includes two staples of Japanese
cooking—tamari (wheat-free soy sauce)
and miso (fermented soy bean paste)—
to give this recipe an Asian twist.
Sesame oil seals the deal (page 146).

Kumquat-Tangerine-Meyer Lemonade (page 163).

Firm tofu that is pressed and then tossed in a mixture of chili oil and sea salt provides some flavorful and satisfying heft to a meal (page 166).

Eaten alone, this 2-rice congee is pretty simple, but an array of accompaniments added to the dish (e.g., tofu with peanuts roasted in chili oil, blanched spinach, shoyu, caramelized onions, and minced cilantro) give it more flavor and complexity (page 164).

A few bites of Gingered Black Sesame-Seed Brittle should be enough to satisfy after a savory meal (page 168).

Velvety Grits with Sautéed Summer Squash, Heirloom Tomatoes, and Parsley-Walnut Pesto

I am very happy when summer squash is in season. I enjoy its subtle flavor and sweet, creamy flesh. When it is at its peak I don't do much to it. Typically, I will sauté it in a small amount of olive oil with a sprinkle of coarse sea salt. One of the keys to making delicious seasonal vegetables is cooking just until al dente. You get the best flavor, and you retain more of the nutrients.

For this dish, I step outside the box and bring together subtle summer squash and heirloom tomatoes with fresh, flavorful pesto atop creamy grits. The combination of these ingredients provides rich unanticipated flavor and a deeply satisfying dish.

Pesto

- 2 cups loosely packed fresh flat-leaf parsley leaves
- 2 medium-size garlic cloves, peeled
- 1 tablespoon mellow white or yellow miso
- ¼ cup freshly squeezed lemon juice
- Coarse sea salt
- ½ cup extra-virgin olive oil
- ⅓ cup walnuts, toasted and skins removed (page 49)

Grits

- 2½ cups water
- 1 cup Vegetable Stock (page 4)
- Coarse sea salt
- ¾ cup grits
- 1 cup unflavored rice milk
- ½ cup Creamed Cashews (page 14)

YIELD
4 to 6 servings

SOUNDTRACK
"Singing in My Soul" by Sister Rosetta Stone from *The Gospel of the Blues*

BOOK
Together We Are One: Honoring Our Diversity, Celebrating Our Connection by Thích Nhất Hạnh

Tomatoes

2 cups medium-diced heirloom tomatoes

¼ teaspoon freshly squeezed lemon juice

½ teaspoon coarse sea salt

Squash

1½ teaspoons extra-virgin olive oil

1 clove garlic, minced

Coarse sea salt

4 cups (½-inch-diced) summer squash

2 tablespoons filtered water

Freshly ground white pepper

For the pesto

In the bowl of a food processor fitted with a metal blade, combine the parsley, garlic, miso, lemon juice, and ½ teaspoon of salt and puree. Slowly add the oil and process until smooth. Add the walnuts and pulse a few times until chunky but incorporated. Set aside.

For the grits

In a medium-size saucepan, combine 2 cups of water, the vegetable stock, and ½ teaspoon of salt and bring to a boil. Whisk the grits into the liquid until no lumps remain, return to a boil, then quickly lower the heat to low. Simmer, stirring frequently to prevent the grits from sticking to the bottom of the pan, until the grits have absorbed most of the liquid and are thickening, 10 to 12 minutes. Stir in the rice milk and simmer for another 10 minutes, stirring frequently, until most of the liquid has been absorbed. Stir in the Creamed Cashews and the remaining water and simmer, stirring frequently, until the grits are soft but not runny, 35 to 40 minutes. Season with salt to taste.

For the tomatoes

Combine the tomatoes, lemon juice, and salt in a mixing bowl and toss well. Set aside.

For the squash

In a medium-size sauté pan over high heat, combine the olive oil, garlic, and ¼ teaspoon of salt and sauté, stirring often, until fragrant, about 2 minutes.

Add the squash and sauté, stirring often to ensure that the squash is well coated with oil, until softening, about 2 minutes. Add the water, cover, and steam until tender, about 2 minute.

Season with salt and white pepper to taste.

For each serving, spoon about ½ cup of the squash and 2 tablespoons to ¼ cup of the tomatoes over ¾ cup of grits. Add a few dollops of pesto to finish it off.

YIELD
4½ cups

SOUNDTRACK
"That Face" by Sarah Vaughn and the
Jimmy Rowles Quintet from *Sarah
Vaughn and the Jimmy Rowles Quintet*

BOOK
I Like Myself! by Karen Beaumont and
illustrated by David Catrow

Frozen Café No Lait with Nutmeg and Chocolate Shavings

*Although I prefer making flavored ice using this old-school method,
you can also freeze the coffee mixture in ice cubes and pulse them in
a food processor in batches until smooth but not slushy. Frozen leftovers can also be pureed in a food processor just until smooth.*

¼ cup raw cane sugar, or to taste, plus more for garnishing

½ teaspoon ground nutmeg

3 cups unflavored rice milk

2 cups strongly brewed best-quality coffee

1 (1-ounce square) unsweetened vegan chocolate, shaved
with a vegetable peeler

Combine the sugar, nutmeg, and the rice milk in a small saucepan
over low heat. Stir well until hot to touch and the sugar is completely dissolved, about 3 minutes. Remove from the heat. Pour
1 cup of the rice milk into a small bowl and set aside to cool. Add
the coffee to the saucepan of rice milk, stir well to combine, and
set aside to cool.

Refrigerate the bowl of reserved rice milk and the saucepan of
the coffee mixture until cold.

Next, transfer the coffee mixture to a 13 x 9-inch casserole dish.
Cover with foil and place flat in the freezer. Let chill for 30 minutes.

With a large spoon, scrape the frozen crystals from the edges and
the bottom of the pan, breaking apart any frozen chunks, and stir
well to create a slushy mixture. Repeat every 30 minutes until the
mixture is frozen and creamy, about 2 hours. Note: immediately

before serving, larger frozen pieces can be broken up by pulsing in a food processor.

Once the ice has solidified, scoop into individual serving bowls, pour 2 to 3 tablespoons of the reserved rice milk on top, dust with sugar, add the chocolate shavings, and serve immediately.

LOS CAMPESINOS DEL MUNDO
APLASTARAN LA GLOBALIZACION

FARM WORKERS OF THE WORLD, UNITE! SMASH THE WTO! 세계의 노동자는 WTO를 탄압한다.

farm fresh

ç

strawberry-basil agua fresca
cinnamon-tamarind agua fresca
smoky tomatoes, roasted plantains, and crumbled tempeh
coconut quinoa
tortillas stuffed with swiss chard, currants, and spicy guacamole
mexican chocolate pudding and agave-coated pepitas

SOUNDTRACK
Clandestino—Esperando La Ultima Ola by Manu Chao
Proxima Estacion: Esperanza by Manu Chao
La Sandunga by Lila Downs
Una Sangre (One Blood) by Lila Downs
Coconut Rock by Ocote Soul Sounds

The food that overflows our market shelves and fills our
tables is harvested by men, women, and children who
often cannot satisfy their own hunger.

—CÉSAR CHÁVEZ

Despite their role in feeding people, it seems that small-scale farmers and
farm workers are constantly under attack. Internationally, the negative effects
of economic globalization on poor farmers have been devastating, and the
high costs of running a farm combined with low profits and debt to agribusi-
ness corporations have generated a global surge in farmer suicides.

Many people became aware of the contemporary struggles of farmers in
2003 when Lee Kyung Hae—a South Korean farmer, former lawmaker, and
activist—took his life during a protest at the World Trade Organization's
Ministerial Conference in Cancún, Mexico. Right before his death, Lee (with

over three hundred South Korean farmers and union activists) was participating in a mock funeral for poor people negatively impacted by the policies of the WTO. He was carrying a banner that read WTO KILLS FARMERS.

Environmental activist Vandana Shiva has a lot to say about the economic exploitation of small farmers in India. In her book *Stolen Harvest: The Hijacking of the Global Food Supply*, she reminds us that the destructive consequences on poor farmers of free trade agreements make it clear that economic globalization tends to benefit the most wealthy and politically powerful countries while plunging poorer countries and their citizens further into poverty. According to a 2011 study released by the Center for Human Rights and Global Justice at New York University Law School, an Indian farmer commits suicide every 30 minutes.

Historically, harmful policies and neglectful governmental institutions have negatively affected American farmers as well. To start, agricultural-based slave labor laid the basis for American economic growth. Throughout the twentieth century, African American sharecroppers and tenant farmers were exploited under feudal-like conditions. And for decades, African American farmers lost significant amounts of land and potential farm income as a result of discrimination by the USDA. During World War II, Japanese farmers in the Central Valley of California (one of the world's most productive agricultural regions) were sent to internment camps and had to quickly sell their land at great financial loss (or had it taken from them). Today, migrant and immigrant agricultural laborers (mostly Latino) receive low wages and face brutal working conditions, sometimes spending ten to twelve hours in fields on blistering-hot days.

As an ethical eater, I believe that it is my responsibility to ensure that "cruelty-free" extends to all living beings. As a citizen I stand up for justice and call for the fair treatment of all the agricultural laborers who ensure we have the most abundant and diverse food supply on the globe.

asianfarmers.org • *ciw-online.org* • *federationsoutherncoop.com*
themeatrix.com • *www.navdanya.org* • *transfairusa.org*

Strawberry-Basil Agua Fresca

Agua fresca, a nonalcoholic beverage that is popular throughout Mexico, literally means "fresh water." Because it is simply water, fresh fruit, and a sweetener, it's actually one of my favorite things to drink. When making agua fresca for myself, I tend to use very little sweetener, to highlight the added fruit. But if I am making it for others I will add a little more sweetener (in fact, I make them a bit oversweetened to balance the melted ice when served). In the summer I like to keep agua fresca handy, so I usually make a gallon at a time, but feel free to adjust and make a quantity that suits you.

YIELD
About 1 gallon

SOUNDTRACK
Justicia by Ocote Soul Sounds and Adrian Quesada from *El Nino y el Sol*

BOOK
Strawberry Fields: Politics, Class, and Work in California Agriculture by Miriam J. Wells

1 cup minced (as finely as possible) basil leaves (from 1 large bunch)

1¼ cups raw cane sugar, or 1 cup agave nectar, or more to taste
Pinch of salt

13 cups filtered water

4 cups packed quartered strawberries

½ cup freshly squeezed lime juice

After removing ¼ cup of the minced basil and setting aside for later use, combine the sugar, salt, 1 cup of the water, and the remaining basil in a small saucepan over low heat. Stir well until hot to the touch and the sugar is completely dissolved, about 3 minutes. Remove from the heat and let sit for at least 30 minutes. Strain through a fine-mesh strainer into a gallon jar or similar receptacle.

While the basil syrup is sitting, combine the strawberries and 2 cups of the water in an upright blender and blend until smooth. Transfer to the gallon jar with the syrup. Add the lime juice along with the remaining minced basil and water. Stir well.

Serve over ice.

YIELD
About 1 gallon

SOUNDTRACK
"Agua Santa" by Ocote Soul Sounds
from *Taurus*

Cinnamon-Tamarind Agua Fresca

Tamarind, which can be found in Latin American and Asian grocery stores, has a sweet-tart flavor and makes a refreshing, strong drink. The cinnamon flavor perks up this drink adding a sweet-fragrant highlight to each sip.

- 1 cup raw cane sugar or agave nectar, or to taste
- 16 cups filtered water
- 1 pound fresh tamarind pods, shelled and veins removed from the fruit
- ½ cup freshly squeezed orange juice

Combine the sugar, water, and the tamarind fruit in a large pot over high heat. Bring to a boil, and immediately lower the heat to medium. Simmer, stirring frequently to incorporate, for 15 minutes. Remove from the heat and let sit for at least 2 hours. Once cooled, fish out the seeds and any remaining strings and shells, leaving the pulp behind (it may be necessary to squeeze seeds from the tamarind pulp). In batches, combine the water and pulp in an upright blender. Blend until well pureed, and strain through a fine-mesh strainer into a gallon jar or similar receptacle. Add the orange juice, and refrigerate until cold.

Serve over ice.

Smoky Tomatoes, Roasted Plantains, and Crumbled Tempeh

SOUNDTRACK
 "Brown Paper People" by Lila Downs
 from *Una Sangre* (*One Blood*)

BOOK
 Cesar Chavez: Autobiography of La Causa

FILM
 One Penny More directed by Shalini Kantayya

This stew, inspired by one of Rick Bayles's recipes, is perfect for using ripe, juicy tomatoes from your home garden. A chipotle chile (from canned chipotle in adobo sauce) gives it a smoky flavor and combines well with the pungent flavor of ten garlic cloves. The crumbled tempeh adds protein and contributes to the stew's thicker consistency. I add ripe plantains for texture and a touch of natural sweetness.

  3 tablespoons extra-virgin olive oil
  1 cup thinly sliced red onions
  1 large chipotle chile, chopped finely (canned)
 10 garlic cloves, peeled and roughly chopped
 3¼ pounds ripe tomatoes, or 1 (28-ounce) can whole
    tomatoes, drained
  2 bay leaves
  4 cups Vegetable Stock (page 4)
    Coarse sea salt
 ½ pound (1 [8-ounce] package) tempeh, crumbled
  2 ripe plantains, cut diagonally into ½-inch cubes
 ½ cup chopped fresh cilantro

In a medium-size saucepan over high heat, combine 2 tablespoons of the olive oil with the onions and chipotle and cook for 2 minutes, stirring frequently. Lower the heat to low and cook, uncovered, for 10 minutes, stirring occasionally. Add the garlic and cook for 5 more minutes.

Preheat the oven to 375°F.

Transfer the mixture to a blender, add the tomatoes, and puree until smooth. Pour back in the saucepan, add the bay leaves, and stir constantly over medium heat until cooked down to a thick consistency, about 10 minutes. Stir in the vegetable stock and 1 teaspoon of salt, plus more to taste if necessary.

Add the tempeh, bring to a boil, cover the pot, lower the heat to low, and simmer for about 45 minutes, until the stew has thickened somewhat.

Meanwhile, in a large bowl, combine the plantains, the remaining tablespoon of olive oil, and ½ teaspoon of salt. Toss well. Transfer the plantains to a parchment-lined baking sheet and roast for about 30 minutes, tossing every 10 minutes to ensure even cooking.

Remove the bay leaves, and transfer the roasted plantains to the stew. Add the cilantro, and simmer for 5 more minutes.

Serve with Coconut Quinoa (recipe follows).

Coconut Quinoa

Quinoa, an ancient South American cereal grain, is higher in protein than any other grain. It tastes great cooked in coconut milk, but it's heavenly after soaking up some of the smoky stew.

YIELD
4 to 6 servings

SOUNDTRACK
"Coconut Rock" by Ocote Soul Sounds and Adrian Quesada from *Coconut Rock*

- 1 cup coconut milk
- 1 cup water
  Coarse sea salt
- 1 cup quinoa, rinsed
- 2 tablespoons dried coconut

In a medium-size saucepan over high heat, combine the coconut milk with the water and ½ teaspoon of salt. Bring to a boil. Add the quinoa and dried coconut and bring back to a boil. Immediately lower the heat to low, cover the pot, and simmer for 20 minutes. Remove from the heat and steam with the lid on for 5 minutes, then lightly fluff with a fork.

YIELD
4 servings

SOUNDTRACK
"La Iguana" by the Chieftains from *San Patricio*

Tortillas Stuffed with Swiss Chard, Currants, and Spicy Guacamole

In addition to helping hold the fried tortilla together, the guacamole contains beneficial fats and carbohydrates that make this dish filling. The bitter, salty taste of the sautéed Swiss chard is balanced by the concentrated sweetness of the currants. The tart orange juice enhances the flavor of the sauté and contrasts well with the rich, buttery guacamole. With each bite of this crunchy tortilla, one gets a complex, satisfying array of flavors.

Guacamole

- 2 ripe Hass avocados, peeled and pitted (reserve the pits)
- 3 tablespoons minced fresh cilantro
- ½ cup diced red onion
- 1 garlic clove, minced
- 1 jalapeño chile, seeded and chopped finely
- 1½ tablespoons freshly squeezed lime juice
  - Pinch of cayenne
- ½ teaspoon coarse sea salt, plus more to taste

Swiss Chard

- Coarse sea salt
- 2 large bunches Swiss chard, finely chopped, rinsed, and drained
- 2 teaspoons extra-virgin olive oil
- 2 garlic cloves, minced
- ⅔ cup dried currants
- ⅓ cup freshly squeezed orange juice

Tortillas

- Extra-virgin olive oil
- 8 fajita-size whole wheat tortillas
- Cilantro sprigs, for garnish
- Your favorite hot sauce, for serving

For the guacamole

In a medium-size serving bowl, combine the avocados and cilantro and, using the back of a spoon, mash the avocados until creamy but textured. Add the remaining ingredients and mix well. Add the pits to the guacamole to prevent rapid browning. Set aside.

For the Swiss chard

In a large pot over high heat, bring 3 quarts of water to a boil. Add 1 tablespoon of salt and let dissolve. Add the chard and cook, uncovered, for 1 minute, until softened.

While blanching the chard, prepare a large bowl of ice water.

Remove the chard from the heat, drain, and plunge it into the bowl of cold water to stop cooking and set the color of the greens. Drain.

In a medium-size sauté pan, combine the olive oil and garlic. Turn on the heat to medium-high, and sauté the garlic for 1 minute. Add the chard, currants, and ½ teaspoon of salt. Sauté for 3 minutes, stirring frequently.

Add the orange juice and cook for an additional 15 seconds. Do not overcook (chard should be bright green). Season with additional salt to taste if needed, and set aside.

For the tortillas

Preheat the oven to 200°F.

In a large nonstick or cast-iron skillet over medium heat, warm 1 tablespoon of the oil. Add 1 tortilla and move it around to make sure it's covered with oil. Sprinkle 2 tablespoons of the sautéed chard on half of the tortilla. Add 2 heaping tablespoons of the guacamole on top of that, and cook for 2 minutes. Fold the tortilla over and press down with a spatula for 15 seconds. Flip over and cook another 30 seconds. The tortillas should be lightly browned on both sides.

Place the tortilla on a baking sheet and put in the oven to keep warm.

Repeat to make eight tortillas, keeping them warm in the oven as they are finished.

Before serving, cut each tortilla in half on a cutting board and serve four halves on a large plate garnished with cilantro. Open each slice and give it a dash of hot sauce.

Mexican Chocolate Pudding and Agave-Coated Pepitas

This silky tofu-based pudding is inspired by the flavor profile of Mexican chocolate pudding. Its delicate chocolate flavor is enhanced by candied pepitas, which offer satisfying texture.

YIELD
4 servings

SOUNDTRACK
"Tiringini Tsitsiki" by Lila Downs from *Una Sangre (One Blood)*

BOOK
Colores de la Vida: Mexican Folk Art Colors in English and Spanish by Cynthia Weill

Agave-Coated Pepitas

- 2 cups raw pepitas
- 1 tablespoon light olive oil
- 3 tablespoons dark agave nectar
- 2 tablespoons raw cane sugar

Chocolate Pudding

- ¼ cup unsweetened coconut milk
- 1 teaspoon ground cinnamon
- ¼ cup dark agave nectar
- ¼ cup unsweetened cocoa powder
- ⅛ teaspoon fine sea salt
- ⅛ teaspoon cayenne
- 1 (¾ pound) package Mori-Nu firm silken tofu (this dessert works best with this brand)

For the agave-coated pepitas

In a large mixing bowl, combine the pepitas with the olive oil and stir until thoroughly coated. Add the agave nectar and stir until thoroughly coated. Then add the sugar and stir until thoroughly coated.

Warm a large, heavy cast-iron skillet to medium-high heat. Add the pepitas, scraping the bowl with a rubber spatula to remove everything, and stir constantly until the pepitas are fragrant and most of the liquid has evaporated, about 1½ minutes.

Transfer the pepitas to parchment paper and quickly spread out, separating them with two forks. Set aside to cool.

For the chocolate pudding

In a small saucepan over high heat, combine the coconut milk, cinnamon, agave nectar, cocoa powder, salt, and cayenne. Bring to a boil. Quickly lower the heat to medium and simmer for 2 to 3 minutes, whisking constantly, until the ingredients are incorporated.

Pour the mixture into in a blender, scraping the sides with a rubber spatula. Add the tofu, and blend until smooth. Transfer the pudding to a wide, shallow bowl, cover with plastic wrap, and refrigerate for at least 2 hours.

Top each serving of pudding with a few heaping tablespoons of agave-coated pepitas.

celebration: chisholm

♀

fiery ginger beer / black star lime

creamy chard soup with tostones

jerk tempeh with cilantro sauce

double garlic rice

purple slaw with toasted pecans

citrus-hibiscus sorbet

SOUNDTRACK

Saata Massagana by the Abyssinians

Marcus Garvey/Garvey's Ghost by Burning Spear

Rebel Music by Bob Marley and the Wailers

Prisoner by Lucky Dube

Equal Rights by Peter Tosh

You make progress by implementing ideas.

—SHIRLEY CHISHOLM

Chuck D, founding member of the pioneering hip-hop group Public Enemy, famously proclaimed that "rap is black America's CNN." While his statement underscored the ability of socially conscious hip-hop songs to provide listeners a window into many of the issues faced by historically marginalized communities (e.g., police brutality, failing infrastructure, and poverty), I think it is important to recognize the role that many progressive hip-hop songs play in providing listeners with information—like a news source—on different aspects of American life (e.g., politics, history, current events, and the like). In fact, I would argue that this genre has produced some of the most gripping narratives on everything from factory farming ("Beef" by Boogie Down Productions) to the looming global water crisis ("New World Water" by Mos Def).

I mention all this because I first heard of Shirley Chisholm in a rap song when I was in eighth grade. That's right. Instead of my learning about this brilliant, history-making congresswoman (the first black woman elected to the United States Congress) and presidential candidate (the first major-party candidate of African descent for president of the United States) in my U.S. history class, I found out about her from Biz Markie in his song "Nobody Beats the Biz." Soon after hearing Biz's line "Reagan is the pres but I voted for Shirley Chisholm," I asked my dad who she was. He said something about her being a strong, smart black woman who ran for president the year Nixon was reelected. I pretty much left it at that and did not really think about Shirley Chisholm until years later.

Then in 2004 I saw *Shirley Chisholm '72: Unbought and Unbossed,* the documentary film about her presidential run, when it was showing at the Brooklyn Academy of Music's Rose Cinema. After going to a matinee showing, I returned to my apartment in Bedford-Stuyvesant—the community that Shirley Chisholm represented for seven terms—and spent the rest of that evening thinking about her legacy. To this day, the only national politician that I have seen speak with as much incisiveness, candor, and audacity as

Shirley Chisholm is Barbara Lee (remember when she was the sole member of Congress to vote against giving George W. Bush the power to wage war against Iraq?). Not coincidentally, Congresswoman Lee volunteered for Chisholm's presidential campaign (coincidentally, she represents my district in Oakland.).

And Shirley Chisholm didn't just talk. She acted boldly. As a congress-woman, she stood up for poor African Americans living in her district. She was one of the founders of the Congressional Black Caucus, and she was a fierce opponent of the Vietnam War. She was also a vocal supporter of equal rights for women, and became one of the founders of the National Organization for Women (NOW). Her most fearless act was running for president at a time when major presidential nominees were, without exception, white and male. She knew she had very little chance of winning. But she wanted to make democracy more representative of all Americans. As she wrote in her book, *The Good Fight,* "I ran for the presidency, despite hopeless odds, to demonstrate the sheer will and refusal to accept the status quo."

Although Shirley Chisholm was born in Brooklyn, she was the daughter of a father from Guiana and a mother from Barbados. In recognition of her heritage, this menu draws on the diverse flavors and staples of Caribbean cuisine. It is not only dedicated to Shirley Chisholm for bravely struggling for equality and justice but to any leaders who defend the rights of the poor, people of color, and women.

YIELD
  4 to 6 servings

SOUNDTRACK
  "Black Star Line" by Brand Nubian
    from *In God We Trust*

BOOK
  Marcus Garvey and the Vision of Africa
    edited by John Henrik Clarke

Fiery Ginger Beer / Black Star Lime

If you want a sweet, spicy, and refreshing nonalcoholic beverage that increases blood circulation and promotes digestion, this is your medicine. Ginger drinks (along with sorrel) are standard in many Caribbean and West African restaurants, but I find that using gobs of white sugar is the typical way of sweetening them. In this recipe I use just enough agave nectar to make the intense ginger flavor palatable. If you want a mellower drink, omit the cayenne.

To make a Black Star Lime, replace the lemon juice with lime juice in a glass of Fiery Ginger Beer, add a shot of dark Jamaican rum, and garnish with a slice of star fruit.

  ½   pound fresh ginger, sliced thinly

  ½   cup filtered water

  ½   cup plus 2 tablespoons organic raw cane sugar or agave
      nectar, or to taste

⅛ to ¼ teaspoon cayenne

  6   tablespoons freshly squeezed lemon juice

  6   cups sparkling water
      Several sprigs of fresh mint, for garnish
      Lemon slices, for garnish

Place the ginger in a food processor fitted with a metal blade. Pulse until completely ground into pulp. Wrap the pulp in cheesecloth and squeeze to extract all the juice (you can squeeze it in your hand in batches if you don't have cheesecloth—just strain the juice when you are done squeezing). It should yield about ½ cup of juice. Immediately transfer to a large pitcher and set aside.

Make a simple syrup by combining the filtered water, sugar, and cayenne in a small saucepan over low heat and stirring well until hot to the touch and the sugar is completely dissolved, about 3 minutes.

Add the simple syrup and lemon juice to the pitcher and stir well. Pour in the sparkling water and *gently* stir to combine.

Serve the drink over ice in canning jars. Garnish with mint sprigs and lemon slices.

YIELD
4 to 6 servings

SOUNDTRACK
"Shirley Chisholm, It Is Time for a Change" from *What If I Am a Woman? Volumes 2: Black Women's Speeches* narrated by Ruby Dee with an introduction by Ossie Davis

BOOK
Unbought and Unbossed by Shirley Chisholm

FILM
Shirley Chisholm '72: Unbought and Unbossed directed by Shola Lynch

Creamy Chard Soup with Tostones

This pureed soup is inspired by the Caribbean side dish callaloo. Traditionally, the primary ingredient of callaloo is either amaranth or taro leaves, and in cases where these plants are not available, water spinach is used. I have heard that as a last resort one can use Swiss chard, which is what I do here. Its mild, delicate flavor works perfectly. There is no standard recipe, as callaloo is prepared differently throughout the Caribbean. Here I make a soup inspired by the dish. The addition of coconut milk gives it a bold, creamy quality and lightens the soup's color (making it appealing to the eyes). To bring texture to the dish I add tostones—slices of unripe (green) plantains that have been fried in oil, flattened, and fried again until crisp and golden brown.

Creamy Chard Soup with Tostones

- 1 tablespoon extra-virgin olive oil
- ½ medium-size white onion, diced (about 1 cup)
- ¾ teaspoon ground cumin, plus more for garnishing
  Pinch of cayenne
  Coarse sea salt
- 2 large garlic cloves, minced
- 1 pound Swiss chard, stem removed, chopped into bite-size pieces
- 5 cups Vegetable Stock (page 4)
- 1½ cups coconut milk
- ¼ cup minced fresh parsley
  Freshly ground white pepper

Tostones

Coconut oil
2 to 4 unripe (green) plantains, cut into 1-inch slices
Fine sea salt

For the chard

In a medium-size saucepan over medium-low heat, warm the oil. Add the onion, cumin, cayenne, and ½ teaspoon of salt and sauté, stirring often, until soft, 8 to 10 minutes. Add the garlic and sauté for about 2 minutes, until fragrant. Add the chard and stock. Bring to a boil, and immediately lower the heat to medium. Cover and simmer until the chard has cooked down, 3 to 5 minutes.

Puree the soup in batches in an upright blender or with an immersion blender. Transfer back to the saucepan, add the coconut milk, and season with salt to taste. Simmer over low heat (avoid bringing to a boil), stirring occasionally, for 30 minutes or so to allow the flavors to marry. Garnish each serving with parsley, white pepper, and a pinch of cumin.

For the tostones

While the soup is simmering, warm the oil in a medium-size skillet over high heat. Fry the plantains in batches until golden brown, 2 to 3 minutes for each side. Transfer them to a paper towel–lined plate to cool. When done frying all the plantains, turn off the heat.

With a meat mallet or another hard flat surface, flatten each fried plantain to a ¼-inch thickness.

Rewarm the oil in the skillet over high heat. Refry the flattened plantains in batches until golden and crisp, about 2 minutes. Transfer them to a paper towel–lined plate and immediately season with salt on both sides.

Serve each bowl of soup with a few tostones for texture.

YIELD
4 to 6 servings

SOUNDTRACK
"Man in the Hills" by Burning Spear
from *Man in the Hills*

BOOK
*Rasta and Resistance: From Marcus
Garvey to Walter Rodney* by Horace
Campbell

Jerk Tempeh with Cilantro Sauce

*Jerk spice is one of the distinctive seasonings of Caribbean cooking.
Because of its robust, spicy flavor, it is perfect for enlivening tofu and
tempeh. I sometimes dredge slices of tofu with a dry jerk seasoning,
then fry it on a skillet. But my favorite way of enjoying jerk is oven-
baking slices of tempeh inside a liquid marinade. I suggest cilantro
sauce as another layer of aromatic flavor to brighten this dish. It also
provides additional juiciness for sopping up with your rice, quinoa,
or other grain.*

Tempeh

- 1 pound tempeh (2 [8-ounce] packages) sliced horizontally into ½-inch fingers
- 1 cup chopped yellow onion
- 3 green onions, white and green parts, sliced thinly
- 3 garlic cloves, minced
- 1 habanero chile, stemmed and minced (use ½ to decrease spiciness)
- 1 teaspoon minced fresh ginger
- 3 tablespoons freshly squeezed lime juice
- 1 tablespoon apple cider vinegar
- 6 tablespoons shoyu
- ¼ cup extra-virgin olive oil
- 1 tablespoon raw organic cane sugar, or 2 teaspoons agave nectar
- 1 teaspoon ground allspice
  Pinch of freshly grated nutmeg
- 1 tablespoon minced fresh thyme
  Pinch of cayenne
- 1 tablespoon freshly ground black pepper
- 1½ cups plus 2 tablespoons Vegetable Stock (page 4) or water

Cilantro Sauce

- 2 garlic cloves, minced
- 3 tablespoons extra-virgin olive oil
- ¼ teaspoon ground coriander
  Coarse sea salt
- 1 cup tightly packed fresh cilantro leaves (about 1 large bunch)
- 2 tablespoons freshly squeezed lemon juice
- ¼ cup water
- ½ jalapeño

For the tempeh

Preheat the oven to 350°F.

In a large baking dish, place the tempeh fingers in one snug layer. Set aside.

In an upright blender, combine the remaining ingredients and puree until well mixed. Transfer the sauce to a small saucepan. Bring to a boil, and immediately pour over the tempeh. Tightly cover the dish with foil, transfer to the oven, and bake for 1 hour, until much of the sauce has been absorbed (turning the tempeh halfway through). Remove the foil and bake for an additional 10 minutes.

For the cilantro sauce

Combine the garlic, olive oil, coriander, and ¼ teaspoon of salt in a small skillet. Raise the heat to medium and simmer just until the garlic is fragrant, about 1½ minutes. Remove from the heat and let cool.

Transfer the oil mixture to an upright blender. Add the cilantro, lemon juice, water, and jalapeño and blend until smooth. If necessary, season with additional salt to taste.

Double Garlic Rice

Before cooking this rice I sauté thin slices of garlic in oil and reserve them for incorporating into the rice immediately before serving. Because the garlic is cooked until almost burnt, it is crunchy, slightly sweet, and mellower than lightly cooked garlic.

- 1 cup long-grain brown rice, soaked in water overnight
- 2 tablespoons extra-virgin olive oil
- 5 large cloves garlic, sliced thinly
- 1 cup diced yellow onion
- 1 large jalapeño, seeded and cut into ¼-inch dice
  Coarse sea salt
- 2¼ cups water

Drain the rice into a colander and set aside.

In a medium-size saucepan, combine the oil and garlic, ensuring that the garlic slices are in one layer. Turn the heat on low and simmer until the garlic is crispy and golden brown, about 5 minutes. Turn off the heat. With a fork, transfer the garlic chips to a paper towel–lined plate, and set aside.

Pour off a little more than 1 tablespoon of the garlic oil, and reserve it for another dish. Add the onion to the saucepan and sauté over medium-low heat until well caramelized, 10 to 15 minutes. Add the rice and cook for about 2 minutes, stirring often, until the water has evaporated and the rice starts to smell nutty. Add the jalapeño and ½ teaspoon of salt and cook until fragrant, about 1½ minutes.

Add the water to the saucepan. Bring to a boil, cover the pot, lower the heat to low, and simmer for 50 minutes.

Remove from the heat and steam with the lid on for at least 10 minutes. Right before serving, add the reserved garlic chips to the rice, then fluff it with a fork before serving, incorporating the garlic chips well.

Purple Slaw with Toasted Pecans

Coleslaw is an American standard during summer, especially at cook-outs. Thing is, most versions are drowned in mayonnaise and sugar. So I created this simple yet satisfying version, inspired by one of Skye Gyngell's salads, as a new standard. It combines red cabbage with grated beets to add a pop of color to any table. The vegetables are complemented by a creamy silken tofu–based dressing. In general, this crunchy salad is juicy and refreshing. But when eaten with this menu, it provides a cooling counterpoint to the spicy jerk tempeh.

YIELD
4 to 6 servings

SOUNDTRACK
"Them Belly Full (But We Hungry)" by Bob Marley and the Wailers from *Rebel Music*

BOOK
The Other Side of Paradise: A Memoir by Staceyann Chinn

½ head large purple cabbage, cored and sliced very thinly into long pieces

1 cup coarsely grated raw beet

2 tablespoons freshly squeezed lemon juice

2 tablespoons apple cider vinegar

1 teaspoon Dijon mustard

½ large garlic clove, minced

¼ cup chopped fresh parsley

½ teaspoon agave nectar

Coarse sea salt

¼ cup silken tofu

2 tablespoons extra-virgin olive oil

Freshly ground white pepper

½ cup chopped toasted pecans

3 Granny Smith apples, cored and sliced thinly

Place the cabbage and beet in a medium-size bowl, and set aside.

In an upright blender, combine the lemon juice, vinegar, mustard, garlic, 2 tablespoons of the parsley, agave, ½ teaspoon of salt, and tofu. Blend while slowly adding the oil. Season with salt and pepper to taste.

Pour just enough dressing over the bowl to moisten the vegetables (reserve the remaining dressing for drizzling on the salad before serving). With clean hands massage the contents of the bowl until wilted, 3 to 5 minutes. Stir in the pecans.

Serve on individual plates by layering an apple slice, topping with slaw, then repeating once, piling it high. Drizzle with dressing, and garnish with parsley.

Season with pepper to taste and serve.

Citrus-Hibiscus Sorbet

Inspired by the popular Caribbean drink sorrel, this dessert is made from dried Hibiscus sabdariffa, *commonly referred to as Jamaican or red sorrel (it should not be mistaken with garden sorrel—*Rumex acetosa). *It is light, beautifully colored, and cooling, and makes a refreshing palate cleanser. It can also be enjoyed as a dessert unto itself—a great way to cap off a meal on a hot summer evening. The juice and zest of the orange along with the lemon juice and vodka complement the hibiscus's citrus overtones well. While this sorbet is tangy, the sugar provides a balancing contrast. You can buy dried sorrel in Caribbean and African specialty stores. But you should ask for dried hibiscus flowers if shopping elsewhere.*

3 cups water

½ cup (about ½ ounce) dried hibiscus

1 cup sugar, or to taste

Zest of 1 medium-size orange

2 tablespoons freshly squeezed lemon juice

½ cup freshly squeezed orange juice

1 tablespoon vodka

In a medium-size saucepan over high heat, combine the water with the hibiscus. Bring to a boil. Lower the heat to medium and simmer, stirring occasionally, for 5 minutes. Add the sugar and stir well until completely dissolved, about 3 minutes. Remove from the heat, cover, and set aside to steep for 1 hour.

Stir in the orange zest, lemon juice, orange juice, and vodka, then refrigerate until cold.

Remove from the refrigerator and add more sugar to sweeten if necessary.

Pour into an ice-cream maker and freeze according to the manufacturer's instructions. Keep in the freezer until ready to serve.

YIELD
About 3½ cups

SOUNDTRACK
"You Are My Angel" by Horace Andy from *Wicked Dem a Burn*

BOOK
Sugar Cane: A Caribbean Rapunzel by Patricia Storace with illustrations by Raúl Colón

detroit harvest

ida b. limeade

*black-eyed peas in garlic-ginger-braised mustard greens
with quick-pickled mustard greens, sesame seeds, and tamari*

black "forbidden" rice with parsley

molasses, miso, and maple candied sweet potatoes

rice wine–poached asian pears with spiced syrup

SOUNDTRACK
Aaliyah by Aaliyah
Welcome 2 Detroit by J Dilla
Detroit Summer/Emergence by Invincible + Waajeed
Statements by Milt Jackson
The White Stripes by the White Stripes

It will become clearer to more millions that our good
health depends on our making the good food revolution.

—GRACE LEE BOGGS

My wife and I are deeply moved by the partnership of Grace Lee Boggs and her late husband, James Boggs. For us, their relationship serves as an example of the immense power of two people sharing fervor for creativity and activism as well as a romantic bond. The fact that they were an Afro-Asian couple makes them that much more relevant to us. More than anything, we are inspired by the impact that they had on progressive radical movements in Detroit and beyond.

I first discovered Grace while I was in graduate school. I learned that she had been active in social change movements throughout the twentieth century—from civil rights to more recent efforts to restore abandoned urban centers in the United States (by the way, she is still, in her nineties, theorizing, writing, and working on grassroots efforts in Detroit). But it was not until I read her autobiography, *Living for Change*, in 2001 that I learned about her relationship and work with political activist and autoworker James Boggs.

They married one year after Grace moved to Detroit in 1953. As a couple they were influential figures in the radical wing of the civil rights movement, they co-authored two books, and in 1992 they founded Detroit Summer—a multiracial, intergenerational collective aimed at transforming Detroit through youth leadership, creative expression, and collective action. Years after reading about Detroit Summer, my friend Ilana (a.k.a. Invincible) told me about her work as a mentor in the collective, and I was happy to hear that it continued to respond to the devastating economic effects of deindustrialization in Detroit. One of the most compelling aspects of Detroit Summer's work is its focus on generating alternative community-controlled systems rather than solely reforming deteriorating old systems.

I was most excited to learn that one of the major focuses of Detroit Summer's early years was food justice. For the collective, creating more access to healthy food was not only important for improving community health but also for building stronger local economies, providing citizens with productive work, and healing the planet. In the mid-1990s, Detroit Summer paired gardening angels—elders growing their own food in neighborhoods—with young people to build hundreds of community gardens for families and communities. In a city where there was not one major grocery outlet, this was a radical act of self-determination.

Detroit has blazed a trail for the good food revolution based in low-income urban centers, and its residents are re-imagining what American cities can look like in the twenty-first century. More and more people are looking to the city as a model for rebuilding historically marginalized communities across the United States and ensuring that all people have access to healthful food. As Invincible reminds us in her song "Detroit Summer," "You call Motown a ghost-town, but the city's vibrant!"

In honor of James and Grace Lee Boggs and the influence they have had on Detroit, these recipes draw on the flavors, staples, and spirit of Afro-diasporic and Asian cuisine. I dedicate this menu to Detroit Summer for bringing people of all races, cultures, and ages together to build power from within communities and create positive change. I send a *Power Fist* to the Detroit Food Justice Task Force and the Detroit Black Community Food Security Network for their work in Detroit's communities of color. And I raise a glass full of Ida B. Limeade to all the resilient and brilliant people living, loving, and learning in communities throughout the D.

RIP J Dilla.

boggscenter.org • *detroitblackfoodsecurity.org*
detroitfoodjustice.org

YIELD
   6 to 8 servings

SOUNDTRACK
   "Strange Fruit" by Nina Simone
   remixed by Tricky and Tool from
   Verve Remixed

BOOK
   A Sword Among Lions by Paula
   Giddings

FILM
   The Show directed by Cruz Angeles

Ida B. Limeade

This limeade is dedicated to one of the fiercest freedom fighters of the twentieth century—Ida B. Wells-Barnett. She was an early leader in the civil rights movement and a vocal anti-lynching activist. She was also instrumental in the women's rights and women's suffrage movements.

The sour juice of freshly squeezed limes is combined with cayenne and raw cane sugar. It is finished off with a tablespoon of beet puree to give this drink a beautiful light fuchsia hue.

  6 cups water

  ½ cup plus 2 tablespoons Simple Syrup (page 30) or agave nectar

  ½ cup freshly squeezed lime juice
     Pinch of cayenne

  1 tablespoon fresh beet juice or Marinated Beets pureed (page 29)

Combine the water, Simple Syrup, lime juice, and cayenne in a pitcher and mix well. Add the beet juice to the pitcher, and let it settle naturally. Place in a freezer until ice cold but not frozen.

Serve ice cold in canning jars.

Black-Eyed Peas in Garlic-Ginger-Braised Mustard Greens with Quick-Pickled Mustard Greens, Sesame Seeds, and Tamari

Because we always have lots of mustard greens growing in our garden, this has become a standard dish in our home. The combination of simmered black-eyed peas and sautéed mustards is simple yet flavorful, and the taste deepens after sitting overnight. I use just enough ginger to provide some warmth and subtle zing without overpowering the dish. Right before serving, finish it off with tamari and a heaping dollop of quick-pickled mustard greens. You can eat this dish alone, but I think you will get the most pleasure by eating it in a bowl along with the black rice and yams in this menu.

YIELD
4 to 6 servings

SOUNDTRACK
"Detroit Summer" by Invincible +
   Waajeed from *Detroit
   Summer/Emergence*

BOOK
Living for Change by Grace Lee Boggs

Black-Eyed Peas

 1 cup dried black-eyed peas, sorted, soaked overnight,
      drained, and rinsed
 1 (3-inch) piece kombu
      Coarse sea salt

Mustard Greens

      Coarse sea salt
 1½ pounds mustard greens, ribs removed and composted,
      leaves coarsely chopped
 3 tablespoons extra-virgin olive oil
 ½ cup finely chopped red onion
 2 teaspoons minced fresh ginger
 ¼ teaspoon red pepper flakes
      Coarse sea salt
 2 garlic cloves, minced
 1 cup Vegetable Stock (page 4)
 1 tablespoon sesame seeds
 2 tablespoons tamari sauce, or more to taste
      Quick-Pickled Mustard Greens (page 19)

Making the black-eyed peas

In a medium-size saucepan over high heat, combine the black-eyed peas with the kombu and enough water to cover them by 4 inches. Bring to a boil. Skim off any foam, lower the heat to medium-low, and simmer, partially covered, just until tender, 50 minutes to 1 hour. Add ¼ teaspoon of sea salt for the last 10 minutes of cooking.

Drain the beans in a colander, reserving 2 cups of cooking liquid. Set the beans and liquid aside.

Making the mustard greens

In a medium-size saucepan over high heat, bring 3 quarts of water to a boil and add 1 tablespoon of salt. Add the greens and boil, uncovered, for 3 to 5 minutes, until softened. Drain in a colander, and set aside.

In a large sauté pan or a medium-size saucepan over medium heat, combine the olive oil, onion, ginger, red pepper flakes, and ¼ teaspoon salt, and sauté, stirring often with a wooden spoon, until softened, 3 to 5 minutes. Add the garlic and cook, stirring often, until fragrant, about 2 minutes. Add the reserved greens and stir to incorporate.

Stir in the vegetable stock, the reserved black-eyed peas, and the reserved bean liquid. Raise the heat to high, and bring to a boil. Cover, lower the heat to medium-low, and cook, stirring occasionally, until the greens are tender, 30 to 45 minutes. Stir in the sesame seeds, season with tamari sauce to taste, and serve along with a whopping dollop of Quick-Pickled Mustard Greens to add some heat and tang.

Black "Forbidden" Rice with Parsley

Black rice, also known as "forbidden" rice, was considered an aphrodisiac in ancient China only to be enjoyed by emperors and their close ones. It has a fragrant aroma, soft texture, and pronounced nutty taste. A few years ago I only saw it being sold in Asian grocery stores and some health food stores. Now it is a lot more common, and I have seen it in a number of conventional supermarkets.

1	cup black "forbidden" rice
2¼	cups water
1	teaspoon extra-virgin olive oil
½	teaspoon coarse sea salt
¼	cup minced parsley

In a medium-size saucepan or a medium-size bowl, combine the rice, water, olive oil, and sea salt. Cover, and refrigerate overnight.

In a saucepan over high heat, bring the rice to a boil. Cover, lower the heat to low, and cook for 50 minutes.

Remove from the heat and steam with the lid on for at least 10 minutes. Before serving, add the parsley, then incorporate by fluffing the rice with a fork.

YIELD
4 to 6 servings

SOUNDTRACK
"Black Is the Color of My True Love's Hair" by Nina Simone and Jaffa from *Verve Remixed 2*

BOOK
Revolution and Evolution in the Twentieth Century by James and Grace Lee Boggs

YIELD
4 to 6 servings

SOUNDTRACK
"Revolution" by Nina Simone from
Protest Anthology

BOOK
*Conversations in Maine: Exploring our
Nation's Future* by James Boggs and
Grace Lee Bogs

Molasses, Miso, and Maple Candied Sweet Potatoes

Candied sweet potatoes is a popular side dish often served on holidays in the South. This everyday version makes use of two staples of Japanese cooking—tamari (wheat-free soy sauce) and miso (fermented soybean paste)—to give this recipe an Asian twist. Sesame oil seals the deal. One might imagine the taste of these strong ingredients overpowering the combination of cinnamon, sugar, molasses, and maple. But the complex, multilayered flavors coexist harmoniously and yield a perfect balance of sweet and savory. The yams are roasted first to caramelize their exterior and bring out their inherent earthy sweetness. Next, the liquid is used to baste the yams for over half an hour to ensure that they are moist. Result: Slammin'.

2½ pounds sweet potatoes or garnet yams, peeled and cut into ½–inch rounds

2 tablespoons toasted sesame oil

1 (2-inch) cinnamon stick

2 tablespoons molasses

1 teaspoon tamari or shoyu

2 tablespoons pure maple syrup

1 heaping tablespoon white or yellow miso

¼ cup freshly squeezed orange juice

1 tablespoon freshly squeezed lemon juice

¼ teaspoon grated lemon zest

6 tablespoons filtered water

Preheat the oven to 425°F.

In a large bowl, toss the yams with 1 tablespoon of the sesame oil.

Spread the sweet potatoes on a parchment-lined or well-greased baking sheet in a single layer and roast for 50 minutes, turning over with a fork after 25 minutes.

Remove the sweet potatoes from the oven and lower the heat to 375°F.

Place the cinnamon stick at the bottom of a 2-quart baking dish, and add the sweet potatoes in layers. Set aside.

In a medium-size bowl, whisk together the molasses, tamari, maple syrup, miso, orange juice, lemon juice, lemon zest, water, and the remaining tablespoon of sesame oil. Pour over the sweet potatoes.

Bake, uncovered, for 30 minutes, thoroughly basting the sweet potatoes every 10 minutes.

YIELD
4 to 6 servings

SOUNDTRACK
"Her Tears Taste Like Pears" by Dorian
Concept from *Her Tears Taste Like
Pears*

BOOK
Red Is a Dragon: A Book of Colors by
Roseanne Thong with illustrations
by Grace Lin

Rice Wine–Poached Asian Pears with Spiced Syrup

One of my favorite ways to take advantage of seasonal pears is to simmer them gently in a combination of wine, water, sugar, and spices—this process is also known as poaching. Asian pears are especially tasty when poached, as they are firm and crisp (as opposed to the buttery texture of Anjou, Bartlett, and Bosc pears). Their starting texture results in a poached pear that is soft but not mushy.

The naturally sweet juiciness of Asian pears nicely complements a sauce made from the reduced poaching liquid. I typically use Riesling as the base, but I wanted to use plum rice wine in this dessert to bolster its Asian flavor profile. When reduced, the poaching liquid resembles a spiced honey. In fact, we use any leftover reduction as a sweetener for oatmeal, grits, and the like.

3 cups plum rice wine (Riesling works just as well)
1 cup water
1 cup raw cane sugar
2 (4-inch) cinnamon sticks
2 star anise pods
1 (½-inch) round fresh ginger
    Zest of 1 medium-size orange, removed in strips with a
    vegetable peeler
5 Asian pears, peeled, cut into quarters, and cored

In a large saucepan over low heat, combine the wine, water, sugar, cinnamon, star anise, ginger, and orange zest. Bring to a simmer. Cook, stirring often, until hot to the touch and the sugar has completely dissolved, about 3 minutes.

Add the pears, raise the heat to medium, and simmer, stirring often, until just tender, 10 to 15 minutes. Remove from the heat.

With a slotted spoon, transfer the pears to a large bowl and re-frigerate to cool.

Over high heat, bring the poaching liquid to a boil. Reduce the liquid until thick and syrupy (to about 1 cup) for 20 minutes or so. Remove the solids from the poaching liquid with a slotted spoon and compost them.

Transfer the syrup to a heatproof bowl and refrigerate until cool.

Serve the pears drizzled with syrup.

Jung Making Instructions

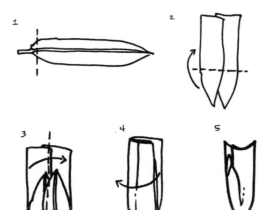

afro-asian jung party
ç

meyer sipping gingerly (my, you're sipping gingerly)
afro-asian jung with shoyu-vinegar-chili sauce
garlic-braised gai laan (chinese broccoli)
chrysanthemum tea, toasted cashews, and persimmons

SOUNDTRACK
Inspiration Information by Mulatu Astatke and the Heliocentrics
Into the Wind by Bei Bei and Shawn Lee
Ethiopiques, Vol. 4: Ethio Jazz & Musique Instrumentale
(1969–1974) by Mulatu Astatke
Lost In Translation by Bei Xu
Silk Road Journeys–When Strangers Meet by Yo-Yo Ma

Jung (*zongzi* in Mandarin) is a simple, balanced, and complete meal of rice, protein, and vegetables wrapped in bamboo leaves. For centuries, jung has provided working people in China and southeast Asia with inexpensive portable food that holds well without refrigeration.

Like tamale making in Mexico, jung wrapping is a skill typically passed down through generations, and my wife and I learned to make them from a friend's mom a few years ago. Since then we have remixed the recipe in endless variations. For our engagement party, we created Afro-Asian jung to symbolize our union: healthy, flavorful, and assembled in the spirit of unifying our two cultures.

We both came to the table deeply rooted in our cultural foodways and excited to create new culinary traditions together, and we see our tastiest meals as microcosms of our histories, remembered through our grandmothers' kitchens. When making Afro-Asian jung, we set out to celebrate the African Americans and Asian Americans who fought side by side in the social justice movements of the 1960s and 1970s; to illuminate the historical moment

151

when Africans and Asians came together in Indonesia at the Afro-Asian Unity Conference of Bandung in 1955 to promote economic and cultural cooperation and to oppose colonialism; and to honor our great-grandfathers who toiled as agricultural laborers and helped build America's wealth.

Although white glutinous rice (also known as sweet or sticky rice) is traditionally used to give jung its trademark stickiness, we used three kinds of rice (black "forbidden" rice, brown glutinous rice, and white glutinous rice) to add color, texture, and depth of flavor. For additional filling, we used peanuts (a staple of African and African American cooking as well as a symbol of long life for Chinese people), black-eyed peas (a symbol of good luck for African Americans), and shiitake mushrooms (a symbol of longevity in China and Japan).

Assembling jung can be time-consuming, so it is best to put them together with a group of people. Making a large batch is a great community-building activity. And once people have a taste, they all agree that the effort was well worth it. My wife and I occasionally have jung-making parties where we invite friends over, provide people with snacks, collectively make jung, eat some together, then divvy up the rest among the group. The general consensus is that having some frozen jung on hand is a great way to ensure that busy people have quickly prepared, hearty food ready to go after a long day.

Meyer Sipping Gingerly
(My, You're Sipping Gingerly)

I created this for the third "issue" of Pop-Up Magazine *in San Francisco, the world's first live magazine (www.popupmagazine.com). I presented about the positive ripple effects that one small action can have, and I demonstrated how to make this cocktail. They served it at a reception after the show. The drink was a big hit, although overly spicy as it is tricky scaling up a cocktail like this. So if serving these at a party, I would designate someone to make them on the spot for each guest.*

If Meyer lemons are not available in your area, regular lemons work just as well. You can buy ginger-infused vodka or you can make it yourself by adding a few 1-inch-thick rounds of ginger to 750 ml of vodka and letting it sit for a few days, agitating occasionally. Look for kaffir lime leaves at an Asian grocery store. If you can't find them, use regular lime leaves. You can always make this drink without lime leaves, but they give it that extra oomph.

3 tablespoons ginger-infused vodka in which 6 to 8 kaffir lime leaves have been soaked overnight

1 teaspoon Sugar-Cayenne Simple Syrup (page 32)

2 tablespoons freshly squeezed Meyer lemon juice

4½ teaspoons sparkling spring water

½ kaffir lime leaf, cut into a chiffonade

Fill a cocktail shaker with ice. Top it with cold water, and place in a freezer. Next, rinse a martini glass with cold water and immediately place in a freezer until chilled, about 5 minutes.

Remove the cocktail shaker from the freezer, empty, and refill with fresh ice. Remove the martini glass from the freezer.

Combine the vodka, Simple Syrup, lemon juice, and spring water in the chilled shaker. Vigorously shake the ingredients until well chilled. Strain into the martini glass.

Garnish with a few strands of kaffir lime leaf.

YIELD

1 serving

SOUNDTRACK

"Esketa Dance" by Mulatu Astatke and the Heliocentrics from *Inspiration Information 3*

BOOK

Afro Asia: Revolutionary Political and Cultural Connections between African Americans and Asian Americans edited by Fred Ho and Bill V. Mullen

YIELD
20 servings

SOUNDTRACK
"Chinese New Year" by Mulatu Astatke
and the Heliocentrics from
Inspiration Information 3

BOOK
*The Color Curtain: A Report on the
Bandung Conference* by Richard
Wright

Afro-Asian Jung with Shoyu-Vinegar-Chili Sauce

This version of jung calls for three different types of rice: black "forbidden" rice, brown glutinous rice, and white glutinous rice. All three can be found at most health food stores and Asian grocery stores. You can find bamboo leaves at Asian grocery stores, too. Feel free to add different ingredients for variation (e.g., diced plantains, chestnuts, or whatever you like). While hearty, the taste of jung is simple after boiling for so long. So don't hold back on the dipping sauce to liven them up.

Jung

40   dried bamboo leaves (plus extras for mishaps)

1   cup black "forbidden" rice, soaked in water overnight

2   cups brown glutinous rice, soaked in water overnight

2   cups white glutinous rice, soaked in water overnight

  Coarse sea salt

5   tablespoons extra-virgin olive oil

1½   cups black-eyed peas, soaked in water overnight

10   shiitake mushrooms (soaked in water overnight if dried)

1   large onion, diced

1½   cups raw peanuts

Dipping Sauce

½   cup minced fresh cilantro

1   jalapeño, seeded and minced

½   cup thinly sliced green onion

½   cup shoyu

2   tablespoons white vinegar

1   tablespoon red wine vinegar

1½   teaspoons raw cane sugar

½   cup water

For the jung

In a large pot over high heat, bring 4 quarts of water to a boil. In batches of four or five, boil the bamboo leaves until they are soft, about 2 minutes. After all the leaves are boiled, rinse them well, transfer them to a container, and cover with water. Discard the water in the pot.

With kitchen scissors, cut the bamboo leaves, widthwise, about ¼ inch below the stem. Discard the stems (diagram 1, page 150).

Drain the rice and combine all three varieties in a large bowl. Add 1 teaspoon of salt and 3 tablespoons of oil and set aside.

Drain the black-eyed peas and set aside.

Drain the shiitake mushrooms and cut each in half.

In a medium-size saucepan over medium heat, combine the onion with 2 tablespoons of oil and sauté until starting to caramelize, about 10 minutes. Add the peanuts and ½ teaspoon of salt and cook until the peanuts start to brown, about 5 minutes. Transfer to a bowl.

Arrange all the ingredients on a worktable. Cut one spool of natural cotton string into sixteen 27-inch-long uniform strands.

Assembling

Line up two bamboo leaves lengthwise, vein side down, placing the left edge of the right leaf flush against the vein of the left leaf. Next, fold the pointed end up one-third the length of the leaves (diagram 2, page 150).

Fold the leaves in half lengthwise (diagram 3, page 150).

Create a pocket for the filling by opening up the fold of the last two leaves on the right (diagrams 4 and 5, page 150).

Holding the pocket at its deepest corner (diagram 6, page 150), insert these ingredients in the following order: 2 tablespoons of the rice mixture, 1 tablespoon of the peanut mixture, 1 tablespoon of black-eyed peas, ½ shiitake mushroom, and 1 more tablespoon of the rice mixture (diagram 7, page 150).

Fold the leaves over the pocket (diagram 8, page 150) and extend the ends of the leaves beyond the edge of the pocket by 1 to 3 inches. The jung should be tightly wrapped, resembling a three-sided pyramid.

Fold down the sides of the leaves to make the last corner of the pyramid (diagrams 9 and 10, page 150). Take the section of folded leaf that overextends the jung and fold it over to one side of the jung (diagram 11, page 150). This is the last fold to close up the corner. It is important that enough of the leaf overextends the jung for you to make these last folds.

During this phase of the wrapping, parts of the bamboo leaves may crack open. If the crack is small (1 inch or less), you can use another bamboo leaf to cover the crack: After making the three-sided pyramid shape, layer the extra bamboo leaf on top of the crack and wrap the rest of the leaf around the pyramid shape.

Tightly wrap a strand of string around one completed pyramid, leaving 4 to 5 inches loose to make the last knot. Start wrapping to secure the last corner fold; this helps to ensure the whole jung stays together as you wrap the rest of it (diagram 12, page 150).

Make a tight double knot (diagrams 13 and 14, page 150).

Repeat until all the jung have been tied.

Cooking

In a large pot over high heat, bring 4 quarts of fresh water to a boil.

Transfer each jung to the boiling water, cover, and cook for 2 hours.

If you have any leftover jung after your meal, they can be frozen and reboiled later.

For the dipping sauce

While the jung are boiling, combine the cilantro, jalapeño, green onion, shoyu, vinegar, sugar, and water in a small bowl. Set aside.

YIELD
4 to 6 servings

SOUNDTRACK
"B4 the Dual" by Benga from *Diary of an Afro Warrior*

Garlic-Braised Gai Laan (Chinese Broccoli)

Gai laan, or Chinese broccoli, is one of my favorite green vegetables. I enjoy its bitter sweetness along with the flavor and body of extra-virgin olive oil. And I have to say that biting into those crunchy stalks is one of the most satisfying experiences that I have when eating vegetables. If Chinese broccoli is not available in your area, your favorite cruciferous vegetable should work in this recipe.

    Coarse sea salt
1   pound gai laan, cut into 1-inch pieces
2   teaspoons extra-virgin olive oil
2   garlic cloves, minced

In a large pot over high heat, bring 4 quarts of water to a boil. Add 1 tablespoon of salt and boil for 1 minute. Add the gai laan, and immediately turn off the heat. Let sit for 1 minute. Drain.

In a large sauté pan, combine the oil with the garlic. Turn the heat on medium, and cook the garlic for about 30 seconds. Add the gai laan and 2 tablespoons of water. Cook until just tender, about 2 minutes.

Dust with salt to taste.

Chrysanthemum Tea, Toasted Cashews, and Persimmons

Sometimes tea, fresh fruit, and nuts are all one needs to cap off a good meal. Purchase food-safe chrysanthemum tea at Asian grocery stores. After drinking, simply refill the pot with hot water for another batch.

Cashews

1 cup raw cashews

Persimmons

6 Fuyu persimmons, cut into quarters (or eighths if bigger)

Chrysanthemum Tea

Water

1½ ounces chrysanthemum petals

For the cashews

Preheat the oven to 350°F.

Spread the cashews on a large parchment-lined baking sheet. Toast for 6 to 8 minutes, stirring halfway through the toasting, until lightly browned.

Set aside to cool.

For the tea

Bring the water to a boil, add the chrysanthemum petals, and steep for 10 minutes.

YIELD
4 to 6 servings

SOUNDTRACK
"Young Toes, Stars and Babies" by 22cats from *She Will Eat You*

BOOK
I Love My Hair! by Natasha Anastasia Tarpley with illustrations by E. B. Lewis

winter in hong kong

☙

kumquat-tangerine-meyer lemonade
2-rice congee with steamed spinach and other accompaniments
tofu with peanuts roasted in chili oil
gingered black sesame-seed brittle

SOUNDTRACK
Placid Places by Alok
She Will Eat You by 22cats
abc by Jin
I Wonder Why My Favorite Boy Leaves Me by the Marshmallow Kisses
Poetic between France and Mong Kok by My Little Airport

I built this meal around one of my all-time favorite winter dishes—a heaping bowl of congee. Congee is all that you would expect it to be by the sound of the word—creamy, soothing, and warming. Come on. Say it with me, slowly (like it's spelled): "Con-gee." Feels good, right? One more time:

"Con-gee." There we go.

My in-laws always referred to this velvety rice porridge as *jook*, its Cantonese name. So it wasn't until I visited Hong Kong and saw CONGEE RESTAURANT signs everywhere that I discovered the dish had another label. We must have eaten congee every day over that two-week trip, mostly for breakfast. At home, however, when the weather is cold my wife and I enjoy it for lunch and dinner as well. It's the perfect comfort food, in my opinion.

Not only is congee comforting, it is also restorative. The most basic recipe only requires rice along with water or stock, making it easily digestible. Like gruel in cultures around the world, congee is served to the ill, plain or garnished with medicinal foods, allowing the body to focus on healing itself.

I am sure you will agree that congee is delicious, too. Alone it is pretty simple, but the array of condiments that are sprinkled over the dish give it more flavor and complexity. It can be enjoyed sweet, but I prefer it savory, adding shoyu, Caramelized Onions, preserved turnips, roasted peanuts, minced cilantro, and fried bread sticks known as *youtiao* (or Chinese dough-nuts, as my wife calls them).

I imagine this menu being enjoyed as a lazy lunch on a Sunday afternoon in the winter. Rather than eating the Tofu with Peanuts Roasted in Chili Oil as a dish unto itself, invite those cubes to the party-in-progress inside the bowl of congee. It's up to you, but I would take my time after eating, let lunch digest, and then have the Gingered Black Sesame-Seed Brittle later in the afternoon.

If preparing this whole menu, start the congee early. Once it is cooked you can always warm it up quickly before the meal. The tofu is done in less than an hour, and assembling the accompaniments for the congee is a cinch.

Kumquat-Tangerine-Meyer Lemonade

Although tangerines are commonplace, many people have never heard of (let alone seen) kumquats, which originated in China. They are cultivated throughout Asia as well as Europe and North America. Most American kumquats come from Florida and California, and they are available during winter months. In case you have never seen them, they look like tiny, oval-shaped oranges. No need to peel them, as one can eat their slightly sweet skin as well as their tart and strong meat. If you can't find kumquats at an Asian grocery store, you can make this drink using only tangerines that have been cut into very thin slices. If Meyer lemons are not available, use plain lemons.

20 to 25	kumquats (½ pound), halved lengthwise
5	tablespoons raw cane sugar
6	cups chilled filtered water
¼	cup freshly squeezed tangerine juice
¼	cup freshly squeezed Meyer lemon juice
3	tangerines, sliced thinly

In a small saucepan, combine the kumquats, sugar, and 1 cup of the water over high heat. Bring to a boil, and stir well until hot to the touch and the sugar is completely dissolved, 3 to 5 minutes. Remove from the heat, and let cool.

Once the kumquat syrup has cooled, transfer the syrup along with the kumquats to a large serving pitcher. Add the remaining water, tangerine juice, and lemon juice and stir well. Add the sliced tangerines, and serve in tumblers.

YIELD
6 to 8 servings

SOUNDTRACK
"Plateau Winter" by Alok from *Placid Places*

BOOK
Tao Te Ching: The Definitive Edition by Lao-tzu, translated by Jonathan Star

YIELD
6 to 8 servings

SOUNDTRACK
"Into the Wind" by Bei Bei and Shawn Lee from *Into the Wind*

BOOK
The Food of China: A Journey for Food Lovers by Kay Halsey and Lulu Grimes, editors, and Jason Lowe, photographer

2-Rice Congee with Steamed Spinach and Other Accompaniments

Although I call for specific additions to this congee, feel free to add whatever your mouth desires that day. Think of the congee as your blank canvas and the accompaniments as a colorful palate from which you create. Because this is a big batch, you can continue experimenting with things to add to the porridge throughout the week (think: breakfast porridge). This recipe starts with uncooked rice, but you can also add water to leftover cooked rice and simmer until it has a creamy texture. It also freezes well, and can be eaten at a later date.

Congee

¼ cup short-grain white rice, soaked in water overnight

¾ cup short-grain brown rice, soaked in water overnight

1 tablespoon peeled, minced, fresh ginger

9 cups Vegetable Stock (page 4)

Freshly ground white pepper

Accompaniments

Shoyu

Toasted sesame oil

Chili oil (page 6)

1 cup Caramelized Onions (page 16)

Quick-Pickled Mustard Greens (page 19)

1 to 2 pounds steamed or blanched spinach (page 70)

2 green onions, thinly sliced

¼ cup minced fresh cilantro

For the congee

Drain the rice and set aside.

In a medium-size saucepan over medium-high heat, combine the rice, ginger, and 6 cups of stock. Bring to a boil, then immediately lower the heat to low and simmer, whisking occasionally, for 30 minutes. Add the remaining stock, and simmer for 2 to 2½ hours more, until the rice is broken up and has the texture of porridge. Whisk the congee vigorously for 1 minute, and season with a few turns of white pepper right before serving.

For the accompaniments

Serve the accompaniments in small bowls along with the congee.

YIELD
4 to 6 servings

SOUNDTRACK
"Learn Chinese" by Jin and Wyclef Jean
from *The Rest Is History*

BOOK
Chinese Feasts & Festivals: A Cookbook
by S. C. Moey

Tofu with Peanuts Roasted in Chili Oil

Roasting is one of my favorite ways to prepare tofu. Because of the resulting firm texture on the outside and creaminess on the inside, it is perfect for layering on a sandwich, adding to a vegetable stir-fry, or eating alongside other dishes. This version, tossed in a mixture of chili oil and sea salt, provides some bold flavor and satisfying heft to any meal. So it seems logical to have it with congee. I also drizzle some of the chili oil on my bowl of porridge for additional heat.

- 2 pounds extra-firm tofu (two large tofu cakes), pressed (see sidebar on left)
- 3 tablespoons Chili Oil (page 6)
- 1 teaspoon fine sea salt
- ¾ cup raw peanuts

Pressing Tofu

Recipes that use firm tofu—as opposed to silken tofu, which is good for nondairy dressings and desserts—often call for it to be pressed. This procedure extracts excess water from tofu and allows it to absorb marinades more easily. It also makes the tofu block more uniformly firm. To press a block of extra-firm tofu, wrap it in several paper towels or a clean kitchen towel, place it in a large bowl or a clean kitchen sink, and place a heavy weight on top for 1 hour, turning after 30 minutes, until most of the liquid is pressed out and absorbed by the towel.

Preheat the oven to 450°F.

Place each tofu cake on its side and cut in half. Lay the cake down flat, keeping the layers together, and cut it, widthwise, into three even slabs. Cut each of those slabs in half widthwise, leaving you with twelve cubes per cake (two dozen total).

In a medium-size mixing bowl, combine the Chili Oil and salt, and mix well with a fork. Add the tofu cubes and *gently* toss to coat with the mixture.

Gently transfer the tofu cubes to a parchment-lined baking sheet in a single layer. Transfer to the oven, and roast for 15 minutes. Reserve the bowl with the remnants of salted chili oil.

Immediately after transferring the tofu to the oven, add the peanuts to the bowl of reserved salted chili oil, toss well, and set aside.

After the tofu has roasted for 15 minutes, *gently* turn each square with a fork. Add the reserved peanuts to the baking sheet with the tofu, and roast for another 15 minutes.

YIELD
About ½ pound

SOUNDTRACK
"Prologue" by the Marshmallow Kisses
from *I Wonder Why My Favorite Boy
Leaves Me an EP*

BOOK
The Frog in the Well by Irene Y. Tsai
with illustrations by Pattie Caprio

Gingered Black Sesame-Seed Brittle

Brittle is a sugary candy that is cooked with nuts to add texture and crunchiness. In China, sesame seeds are used in a range of desserts, so I add them to this brittle, giving each delicate bite rich, nutty flavor and subtle crunch. This dessert should be enjoyed in small amounts, as it is very sweet. A few bites with hot herbal tea after a savory meal is enough to satisfy my sweet tooth. Store in an airtight container.

- 2 tablespoons light olive oil, plus more for oiling the parchment paper
- ⅓ cup black sesame seeds (brown work just as well)
- ½ teaspoon powdered ginger
- ¾ cup raw cane sugar
- 2 tablespoons maple syrup
- 1 teaspoon freshly squeezed orange juice
- ¼ cup filtered water
- 1 teaspoon toasted sesame oil

Line a baking sheet with parchment paper, oil lightly with the olive oil, and set aside.

In a small bowl, toss the sesame seeds with the ginger, and set aside.

In a medium-size saucepan over high heat, combine the sugar, maple syrup, orange juice, and water. Stir constantly until hot to the touch and the sugar is completely dissolved, about 3 minutes. Continue boiling, avoiding stirring or swirling, until a medium amber caramel forms (between 270° and 280°F if using a candy thermometer), about 3 more minutes.

To determine whether the brittle is almost done, take some out with a spoon and set it on the stove. It should harden (soft crack stage).

Remove from the heat, and immediately swirl in the remaining olive oil, sesame oil, and reserved gingered sesame seeds.

Immediately scrape the brittle onto the prepared baking sheet and quickly spread it with a rubber spatula into a very thin layer.

Let cool completely, about 20 minutes, then crack it into shards.

Leave at room temperature in an airtight container for up to 1 month.

fête before fast

slurricane shooter

sour orange daiquiri

ronald dorris

cajun-creole-spiced mixed nuts

gumbo zav

roasted winter vegetable jambalaya

red beans with thick gravy and roasted garlic

café brûlot lace cookies

SOUNDTRACK

Our New Orleans Heart by Mike Molina

It's Our Time to Celebrate by the New Orleans Jazz Ramblers

Yesterday You Said Tomorrow by Christian Scott

New Orleans Ladies by Irma Thomas, Leona Buckles, and Martha Carter

Community is my focus; the gardens are a means to build community.

—JENGA MWENDO, FOUNDING DIRECTOR
OF THE BACKYARD GARDENERS NETWORK,
NEW ORLEANS, LOUISIANA

I think it is only fitting that I end this book with a menu dedicated to New Orleans. When people from Africa, Western Europe, Asia, and the Caribbean commingled with indigenous North Americans in Louisiana, folks of different cultures from around the globe negotiated foodways to create some of the most delectable cuisine the New World had ever seen. Discovering New Orleans's rich culinary history was one of the most important parts of my educational experience as a college student living there, and to this day the

171

Cajun and Creole flavors of the Big Easy have influenced the culinary palette from which I constantly draw. In fact, it can be argued that the core of my cooking style reflects the mixing and mingling of cultural and cooking practices that form the basis of New Orleans cuisine.

As I explain in *Vegan Soul Kitchen*, I imagine "recipes through the prism of the African diaspora—cutting, pasting, reworking, and remixing African, Caribbean, African American, Native American, and European staples, cooking techniques, and distinctive dishes." This approach is not only an effort to creatively make use of the cuisines that tell the story of who I am but it is also an attempt to tell a new story about humanity. Yes, the diversity, beauty, and contrasts of my cooking represent my best hopes and dreams for us all.

Slurricane Shooter

A cup of courage to get the party crunk . . . This shot is a condensed version of the official cocktail of Mardis Gras in New Orleans—the Hurricane. A few of these at the beginning of the night and you'll feel seven feet tall. Dedicated to the homie Mike Fire Esq.

YIELD
1 shot

SOUNDTRACK
"6 Foot 7 Foot" by Lil Wayne featuring Cory Gunz from *Tha Carter IV*

1 tablespoon dark rum

1 tablespoon light rum

1 tablespoon passion fruit nectar juice

1 teaspoon freshly squeezed lime juice

In a shot glass, layer the ingredients as listed. Take it to the head.

YIELD
1 serving

SOUNDTRACK
"I Was The One" by Renée Wilson
from *Voodoo Queen*

Sour Orange Daiquiri

If the Hurricane is the official cocktail of Mardis Gras in New Orleans, then the frozen daiquiri is the official drink of new-to-the-city-college-students-trying-to-get-f****d-up. With dozens of drive-through daiquiri shops scattered New Orleans (yes, you can pull up to a window, purchase an alcoholic beverage, and drive off), and lax enforcement of the minimum drinking age laws (at least in the mid-'90s), getting a sugary-sweet frozen daiquiri was as easy as buying a soda. Here is a more sophisticated version of this rum-based cocktail.

- 2 tablespoons light rum
- 1 tablespoon Cointreau or Grand Marnier
- 2 teaspoons freshly squeezed orange juice
- 2 teaspoons freshly squeezed lime juice
- 1 teaspoon Simple Syrup (page 30)
  Lime slice, for garnish

Shake all the ingredients with ice in a cocktail shaker and strain into a chilled cocktail glass. Garnish with a slice of lime.

Ronald Dorris

This nonalcoholic drink is dedicated to Dr. Ronald Dorris, a brilliant scholar and professor who grew up in the cane fields of Garyville, Louisiana, in St. John the Baptist Parish. Dr. Dorris had a tremendous impact on my intellectual growth in college. He is a true gem of the Xavier University of Louisiana community.

1	teaspoon fine sea salt, for rim of glass
¼	cup raw cane sugar, for rim of glass
½	lime, for rim of glass
½	cup passion fruit nectar juice
1	tablespoon freshly squeezed lime juice
¾	cup sparkling mineral water
	Sugar cane swizzle stick

Fill a cocktail shaker with ice. Top it with cold water, and place it in the freezer. Next, rinse a pint-size canning jar with cold water and immediately place in the freezer.

Remove the cocktail shaker from the freezer, empty, and refill with fresh ice.

Stir the salt and sugar together in a small saucer. Remove the canning jar from the freezer, rub the lime half around the rim, and dip the glass into the sugar mixture to coat the rim.

Combine the passion fruit juice and lime juice in the chilled shaker. Vigorously shake the ingredients until well chilled. Strain into the canning jar.

Top with the sparkling water and garnish with the sugar cane swizzle stick.

YIELD

1 serving

SOUNDTRACK

"From the Plantation to the Penitentiary" by Wynton Marsalis from *From the Plantation to the Penitentiary*

BOOKS

Cane by Jean Toomer

The Sugar Masters: Planters and Slaves in Louisiana's Cane World, 1820–1860 by Richard Follett

YIELD
4 cups

SOUNDTRACK
"On Peanut's Playground" by Wynton
    Marsalis and Ellis Marsalis from *Joe
    Cool's Blues*

BOOK
Purgatory Stories by Michael Molina

Cajun-Creole-Spiced Mixed Nuts

*This mélange of nuts are coated in a zesty spice mixture. I add maple
syrup for a touch of sweetness.*

- 1 cup raw shelled peanuts without skin
- 1 cup raw pecans
- 1 cup raw walnuts
- 1 cup raw almonds
- 2 teaspoons onion powder
- 1 teaspoon garlic powder
- 2 teaspoons paprika
- 2 teaspoons chili powder
- ¼ teaspoon cayenne
- 1 tablespoon pure maple syrup
- 1 teaspoon fine sea salt
- 3 tablespoons extra-light olive oil

Preheat the oven to 350°F.

Spread the nuts in an even layer on a parchment-lined baking sheet.
Bake, stirring every 5 minutes to ensure even roasting, until starting
to crisp and become fragrant, about 20 minutes.

While the nuts are roasting, combine the onion powder, garlic powder, paprika, chili powder, cayenne, maple syrup, and salt in a small
bowl and mix well. Set aside.

Place the olive oil in a large mixing bowl. Transfer the roasted nuts
to the bowl and stir well to coat. Add the spice blend to the bowl and
stir well to coat. Transfer the nuts back to the baking sheet and roast
for 5 more minutes.

Remove from the oven and let cool for 15 minutes before eating.

Store in an airtight container in the refrigerator

Gumbo Zav

This dish is a riff on my Gumbo Z recipe in Vegan Soul Kitchen. *That recipe has been such a hit, I felt compelled to remix it for this book. Gumbo Zav, also known as Gumbo z'Herbes, was traditionally eaten as a nonmeat dish during the Roman Catholic season of Lent. In addition to roux, which is used in many traditional gumbos as a thickener, Gumbo z'Herbes included a combination of several greens (sometimes up to nine), along with other vegetables and spices.*

YIELD
6 to 8 servings

SOUNDTRACK
"American't" by Christian Scott from
Yesterday You Said Tomorrow

BOOK
*Africans in Colonial Louisiana: The
Development of Afro-Creole Culture in
the Eighteenth Century* by Gwendolyn
Midlo Hall

Coarse sea salt

1 large bunch collard greens (about 1 pound), trimmed and chopped finely

1 large bunch mustard greens (about 1 pound), trimmed and chopped finely

1 large bunch kale (about 1 pound), trimmed and chopped finely

1 large bunch spinach (about 1½ pounds), trimmed and chopped finely

½ cup extra-virgin olive oil

7 garlic cloves, minced

½ cup whole wheat pastry flour

2 large yellow onions, cut in ¼-inch dice

¼ teaspoon cayenne

6 cups Vegetable Stock (page 4)

1 teaspoon dried thyme, or 1 tablespoon minced fresh

1 teaspoon filé

1 tablespoon apple cider vinegar

2 large green onions, sliced thinly, for garnish

Your favorite hot sauce

In a large pot over high heat, bring 4 quarts of water to a boil. Add 1 tablespoon of salt.

Add all the leafy greens to the water, bring back to a boil, and cook, uncovered, for 3 to 4 minutes, until softened. Drain in a colander and let cool.

Transfer the greens to a cutting board and chop well.

Combine ¼ cup of the olive oil with the garlic in a large sauté pan over medium heat and sauté until fragrant and starting to turn golden, about 2 minutes. Add the greens mixture, raise the heat to high, sprinkle with 1 teaspoon of salt, and sauté, stirring occasionally, for 2 to 3 minutes, until well coated with oil. Set aside.

In a large pot over low heat, combine the flour and the remaining ¼ cup of olive oil and cook, stirring often with a wooden spoon, until caramel colored, about 25 minutes. Add the onions, cayenne, and ½ teaspoon of salt. Raise the heat to medium and sauté, stirring occasionally and scraping the bottom of the pot, until the onions soften, about 15 minutes. Slowly stir in the stock. Add the greens, bring to a boil, and lower the heat to low. Cover and simmer until meltingly tender, about 45 minutes.

Filé

Filé is simply leaves of a sassafras tree, ground into a fine powder. In addition to roux, filé is used as a thickener in gumbo and other Cajun-Creole dishes. Make sure you add it at the end of cooking, as it becomes stringy if cooked.

Stir in the thyme and simmer for an additional 2 minutes. Remove from the heat, stir in the filé and the apple cider vinegar, and set aside to cool for 10 minutes.

Serve garnished with green onions and hot sauce, along with rice.

Roasted Winter Vegetable Jambalaya

Jambalaya, a Louisiana Creole rice dish, typically includes sausage, seafood, vegetables, and spices. In this version I add roasted root vegetables for heartiness and caramelized sweetness. It is assumed that the Spanish rice dish paella influenced jambalaya, as Spain controlled Louisiana from 1764 to 1803. Being that the Moors of North Africa established the custom of eating composed rice dishes in Spain, I recognize jambalaya's African origin as well.

YIELD
4 to 6 servings

SOUNDTRACK
"Forty Lashes" by Wynton Marsalis
    from *Blood on the Fields*

BOOK
*Soul by Soul: Life inside the Antebellum
    Slave Market* by Walter Johnson

1 cup diced yellow onion
1 teaspoon paprika
½ teaspoon chili powder
¼ teaspoon cayenne
    Coarse sea salt
3 tablespoons extra-virgin olive oil
1 cup long-grain brown rice, soaked in water overnight
    then drained
2 teaspoons tomato paste
3 cups Vegetable Stock (page 4)
1 cup chopped canned tomatoes with their juice
1 cup peeled and ¼-inch-diced carrots
1 cup peeled and ¼-inch-diced parsnips
1 cup peeled and ¼-inch-diced sweet potatoes
1 cup peeled and ¼-inch-diced yellow potatoes
2 teaspoons dried parsley, or ½ cup fresh, chopped
    Freshly ground black pepper

Preheat the oven to 450°F.

Combine the onion, paprika, chili powder, cayenne, ¼ teaspoon of salt, and 2 tablespoons of the olive oil in a large, deep skillet over low heat. Sauté, stirring often, until soft, 5 to 8 minutes. Add the rice, raise the heat to high, and cook for about 2 minutes, stirring often, until the water has evaporated and the rice smells nutty. Add the tomato paste, and stir well to combine.

Stir in the stock and the tomatoes along with their juices, bring to a boil, and immediately remove from the heat. Set aside.

In a medium-size bowl, combine the vegetables, remaining olive oil, and ½ teaspoon of salt.

Transfer the vegetables to a large, parchment-lined roasting pan and roast for 40 minutes, stirring every 10 minutes for even roasting.

Once the vegetables are roasted, transfer them to the rice mixture. Stir to incorporate well, bring to a boil, cover, and lower the heat to low. Simmer until most of the liquid is absorbed, about 50 minutes. Remove from the heat and steam with the cover on for at least 10 minutes.

Before serving, stir in the parsley and season with salt and pepper to taste.

Red Beans with Thick Gravy and Roasted Garlic

Every time I make red beans and rice I feel nostalgic for the years I spent living in New Orleans. In the Big Easy, this dish is ubiquitous—from Grandma's home kitchen to the dining room of Dooky Chase, Leah Chase's famed restaurant in New Orleans' Fifth Ward. In this version I puree 2 cups of the beans along with Roasted Garlic to give the finished dish a rich, thick texture and an earthy, sweet flavor. The minced thyme added at the end provides an aromatic, floral lift to the dish. Eat these beans as they should be eaten, along with rice.

- ½ cup finely diced red onion
- 1 tablespoon extra-virgin olive oil
- 2 cups dried red kidney beans, sorted, soaked overnight, drained, and rinsed
- 1 (3-inch) piece kombu
  Coarse sea salt
- 2 cups Vegetable Stock (page 4)
- 1 head of Roasted Garlic (page 18)
- ¼ cup minced fresh thyme

Combine the onion with the olive oil in a medium-size sauté pan over medium-low heat and cook for 5 to 7 minutes, stirring often, until the onion is soft.

Meanwhile, combine the beans, kombu, and enough water to cover them by 2 inches in a medium-size saucepan over high heat and bring to a boil. Skim off any foam. Quickly lower the heat to medium-low.

Add the sautéed onion to the pot of beans and simmer, partially covered, until tender, 1½ to 2 hours. Stir occasionally to prevent sticking.

YIELD
4 to 6 servings

SOUNDTRACK
"The Uprising" by Christian Scott from *Anthem*

BOOK
American Uprising: The Untold Story of America's Largest Slave Revolt by Daniel Rasmussen

When the beans are almost done, add 1 teaspoon of salt and the stock and stir well to incorporate.

Transfer 2 cups of the cooked beans and their liquid to an upright blender. Add all of the roasted garlic cloves, and blend until creamy, adding more liquid from the pot of beans if necessary. Pour this mixture back into the pot of beans.

Continue cooking the beans, partially covered, for an additional 30 minutes.

Add the thyme and simmer for an additional minute. When reheating, add more stock or water for a thinner texture.

Café Brûlot Lace Cookies

Café Brûlot is a traditional New Orleans after-dinner drink that is hot, strong, and flavorful. Here, I offer lace cookies—dainty drop cookies with lacelike holes—that draw inspiration from the flavors of this Creole classic: coffee, citrus, cinnamon, and cloves. Although brandy is a prominent ingredient in the drink, I choose to leave it out of this cookie as I'm not crazy about alcohol in desserts. But if you'd like to "kick it up a notch," as my friend Emeril Lagasse would say, you can replace 1 tablespoon of the rice milk with 1 tablespoon of brandy. Bam.

YIELD
Approximately 4 dozen cookies

SOUNDTRACK
"I'm Waiting (To Give You My Love)" by Leona Buckles from *New Orleans Ladies*

BOOK
Baby Dance by Ann Taylor with illustrations by Marjorie Van Heerden

1½   cups rolled oats

2   tablespoons whole wheat pastry flour

½   teaspoon ground cinnamon

4   pinches of ground cloves

6   tablespoons coconut butter or oil

½   cup raw organic cane sugar

¼   cup pure maple syrup

2   tablespoons rice milk

2   teaspoons finely ground coffee

⅛   teaspoon orange extract

½   teaspoon finely grated orange zest

½   teaspoon finely grated lemon zest

¼   teaspoon fine sea salt

Preheat the oven to 375°F and grease two large baking sheets, or line with parchment paper.

In a medium-size mixing bowl, whisk together the oats, flour, cinnamon, and cloves. Set aside.

In a medium-size saucepan over low heat, melt the coconut butter if necessary. Stir in the sugar, maple syrup, coffee, orange extract, orange zest, rice milk, lemon zest, and salt until well blended.

Combine the dry mixture with the wet mixture and stir until well combined and smooth in texture.

Drop the dough by teaspoonfuls about 4 inches apart onto the baking sheet. Bake until lightly browned, 12 to 14 minutes.

thanks

Creator.

Ancestors.

Jidan, thank you for being such a loving wife, supportive friend, and creative collaborator. I really appreciate how much you took care of the baby those first seven weeks while I was writing, testing recipes, and editing. I love you.

Mila Bear, I wrote this book for you. Analyze it carefully: Read the books, watch the films, listen to the music, and enjoy the food. Baba loves you very much.

Mom, Dad, and Jay.

Mama Wong and Baba Koon.

Danfeng, Jando, Chencheo, and Alani.

Bryant Clan. Terry Clan. Wong Clan.

team

Danielle Svetcov and everyone at Levine Greenberg Literary Agency. Sally Itterly and everyone at the Lavin Agency. Renée Sedliar (you are the best). Kate Burke (and Wendie Carr). Alex Camlin (genius. pure genius). John Radziewicz. Da Capo/Perseus. Jennifer Martiné. Karen Shinto. Dani Fisher. Nicole Rosario. Fanny Pan. Jonie Noie.

for your support of this book

Leah Katz-Ahmadi. Adrienne Brown. Tamara Chukes. Rachel Cole. Brett Cook. Pete Dosanjh. Nina Fallenbaum. Joshua Gabriel. Polly Green. Charlie Hallowell/Pizzaiolo. Jenny Howard. Shantel Wright-Hines. Alisha Norris Jones. Kalalea. Krys Kagan. Keri Keifer. Rachel Konte. Dani Mcclain. Andrea McKinnon. Verun Mehra. Mike Molina. Alissa Nelson. Alice O'Dea. Amy Pierson. Favianna Rodriguez. Trudy Schafer. Savannah Shange. Rebecca Stevens. Richard Stringfellow. Hallie Montoya Tansey. Robert Trujillo. Renita C. Walker. Lowrie Ward. Alice Waters. Ilana Weaver. Polly Nearman Web.

index

about bryant

Bryant Terry is a chef, food justice activist, author of *Vegan Soul Kitchen: Fresh, Healthy, and Creative African-American Cuisine*, and co-author of *Grub: Ideas for an Urban Organic Kitchen* (which was called ingenious by the *New York Times*). In regard to his work, chef Alice Waters says, "Bryant Terry knows that good food should be an everyday right and not a privilege." For the past decade he has worked to build a more just and sustainable food system and has used cooking as a tool to illuminate the intersections of poverty, structural racism, and food insecurity. His interest in cooking, farming, and community health can be traced back to his childhood in Memphis, Tennessee, where his grandparents inspired him to grow, prepare, and appreciate good food.

Bryant has made dozens of national radio and television appearances, including being a guest on *The Martha Stewart Show*, *Emeril Green*, *The Splendid Table*, and *The Tavis Smiley Show*. He was also a host on the first season of *The Endless Feast*, a thirteen-episode public television series. Bryant contributes essays and recipes to a number of online and print outlets, and his work has been featured in *Food and Wine*, the *New York Times Magazine*, *Essence*, *Yoga Journal*, *Vegetarian Times*, and many other publications. Bryant regularly speaks at public events as well as at colleges and universities such as Brown, Columbia, NYU, Smith, Stanford, and Yale.

Bryant has garnered many honors and awards for his work. From 2008 to 2010 he was a fellow of the Food and Society Policy Fellows Program, a national program of the W. K. Kellogg Foundation. He was selected as one of the 2008 "Hot 20 Under 40" in the San Francisco Bay Area magazine *7x7*. In 2007 he received the inaugural Natural Gourmet Institute Award for Excellence in Health-Supportive Food Education.

In 2002, Bryant founded b-healthy! (Build Healthy Eating and Lifestyles to Help Youth), a multiyear initiative designed to empower youth to be active in creating a more just and sustainable food system. Along with Ludie Minaya, Elizabeth Johnson, and Latham Thomas, Bryant helped elevate cooking as an important tool for organizing and base building in the food justice movement. Bryant completed the chef's training program at the Natural Gourmet Institute for Health and Culinary Arts in New York City. He holds an M.A. in American History from New York University and a B.A. with honors in English from Xavier University of Louisiana.

Bryant lives and creates in Oakland, California, with his wife and daughter.

www.bryant-terry.com • *twitter.com/bryantterry*

contributing artists

photographer

Jennifer Martiné: www.jennifermartine.com (Nicole Rosario)

food stylist

Karen Shinto: www.kshinto.com (Fanny Pan)

prop artist

Dani Fisher: www.danifisher.com (Jonie Noie)

artists

Brett Cook is an artist, educator, and healer. His creative practice includes making dynamic artworks based in portraiture that honor the best of humanity in all of us. In his collaborative practice he employs mindful interpersonal dialogue, participatory pedagogy, and contemplative curricula to facilitate rituals and to build environments where other people make things—and "things" include objects, ideas, and new ways of being. His body of work spans the continuum between the extremes of "solitary" artist and community catalyst, both as one signature and with countless hands skillfully working to relieve suffering in the world. **www.bret-cook.com**

Rachel Konte has a degree in fashion design from the Danish School of Design in Copenhagen and eighteen years of experience working in the apparel industry, most recently as design director at Levi Strauss & Co. She has also worked as a part of the Levi's Red Tab Women's Team and as the design manager for Tommy Hilfiger Denim in Amsterdam. Rachel currently runs her own creative design consulting business, Cirkel Studio, based in Oakland, California (**www.cirkelstudio.com**). She is a co-owner of Guerilla Café in

Berkeley, California (**www.guerillacafe.com**), and her latest project is OAKOLLECTIV a trendy pop-up store in the heart of downtown Oakland (**oakollectiv.blogspot.com**).

Jidan Koon is an organizational development consultant and visual artist who supports social justice organizations in doing their work intentionally, joyfully, and creatively. Currently a senior fellow at the Movement Strategy Center, she brings over fifteen years of on-the-ground experience with organizing and institutional reform to her consulting practice that focuses on leading planning processes and facilitating gatherings. As a visual artist, Jidan creates using a variety of mediums, including painting, illustration, mosaic, collage, and jewelry design. She has collaborated with schools and community organizations to design murals and other public art with children, youth, and adults. **www.jidan-koon.com**

Favianna Rodriguez is a visual artist and new media organizer who has helped foster resurgence in political art both locally and internationally. Hailed as "visionary" and "ubiquitous," Rodriguez is renowned for her vibrant posters dealing with issues such as war, immigration, globalization, sustainability, and social movements. **www.favianna.com**

Robert Trujillo is a storyteller who uses paper, canvas, and walls to speak. His intention is to tell his personal story and collaborate with like minds to tell our collective story. He is a father who regularly dreams about love, being present, diversity in art, good food, good music, and revolutionary change. **www.robdontstop.com**

Marilyn P. Wong is a physician by training. She dabbles in paper and fabric projects for personal enjoyment.

art credits

page **38**: Rosa Lee Terry and Andrew Johnson Terry as young people, circa 1935, photographer unknown

page **50**: *Free Breakfast for Children*, 2004, ink on prepared polyester, by Brett Cook

page **62**: *Arundhati Roy*, 2011, pen and ink on paper, by Rachel Konte

page **74**: *Auntie Alice and Baby Mila*, 2011, photograph by Bryant Terry

page **87**: *Mila*, 2011, collage by Marilyn P. Wong

page **98**: *Thay*, 2004, ink on prepared polyester by Brett Cook

page **112**: *Hermano Kyang Hae Lee*, 2003, screenprint by Favianna Rodriguez

page **125**: *Ms. Chisholm*, 2011, pen and ink on paper, by Robert Trujillo

page **138**: Grace Lee Boggs and James Boggs, circa 1970, photographer unknown

page **150**: *Jung Making Instructions*, 2010, pen and ink on paper, by Jidan Terry-Koon

page **160**: *Food Stand in Macau*, China, 2009, photograph by Marilyn P. Wong

page **170**: *Rue Bourbon*, 2007, aerosol and acrylic on canvas, by Jidan Terry-Koon